A World of Plants

A World of Plants

Treasures from

The Royal Botanic

Gardens, Kew

Heather Angel

A Bulfinch Press Book
Little, Brown and Company
BOSTON • TORONTO • LONDON

NOTE

With the exception of the opening pictures for chapters 2–7,
which depict wild plants in their natural environment
so as to give a taste of the ecosystem relevant
to that particular chapter, all photographs were taken
at the Royal Botanic Gardens, Kew.

BACK FLAP: Photograph of Heather Angel taken by Giles Angel
FRONT COVER: Aechmea fasciata *var.* fasciata
BACK COVER: *Top left:* Androcymbium europaeum;
top right: Aechmea nidularoides;
bottom left: Barbados pride, Caesalpina pulcherrima;
bottom right: Echeveria umbricata
HALF–TITLE: *Joseph's coat or croton,* Codiaeum variegatum 'pictum', *and cycads*
TITLE PAGE: *Detail of pineapple flower,* Eucomis comosa

CONTENTS

CHAPTER ONE

PAST AND PRESENT

*Originally an eighteenth-century
royal estate, The Royal Botanic Gardens, Kew,
now contain one of the largest
collections of living plants anywhere in the
world, with flora from habitats as
diverse as tropical forests, deserts and coral reefs.*

KEW MEANS different things to different people. To most of the one million-plus visitors who come to The Royal Botanic Gardens each year, the 120 hectares (300 acres) represent a green oasis in the city and a pleasant place for a day out. To gardeners and landscape designers the Gardens provide inspiration; to artists and photographers alike they offer a galaxy of colours, shapes and forms. Yet how many visitors pause to consider the way in which plants from far-flung corners of the globe came there? Perhaps few appreciate that many have been collected on numerous expeditions originating from Kew, dating from as far back as the latter part of the eighteenth century up to the present day when plants new to science continue to be found.

For the many scientists who work at Kew, the Gardens provide a rich source of research material – a living laboratory. Indeed, the primary functions of Kew's plant collections are scientific research and education. As well as the Living Collections in the grounds, plants are raised and propagated in extensive nurseries, while a wealth of research material is stored in the Herbarium on Kew Green and in the World Seed Bank at Wakehurst Place – 'Kew in the country' – at Ardingly in Sussex.

The statistics are perhaps even more impressive, for Kew has the world's largest collection of living plants: 83,000 accessions of some 38,000 species, from habitats as diverse as the steamy Amazonian rainforest, the heights of Mount Kenya or the tropical waters around coral reefs. In addition, with

LEFT: *Silhouetted by early morning winter sun, branches
of a Chinese catalpa,* Catalpa ovata, *frame the
Temperate House. This is one of several catalpas,
grouped near the north end of the Temperate House,
which produce attractive panicles of foxglove-like flowers
after the trees are well leafed out in late summer.*

more than six million preserved specimens of seed-producing plants, ferns and larger fungi in the Herbarium, it can justly claim to house the world's most comprehensive collection of plant material. What is more, this collection continues to grow as some 45,000 specimens are added annually.

Kew Gardens are sited on a flood-plain terrace of gravel brought down by the waters of the River Thames. Gradually, as layers of detritus built up, herbs, shrubs and trees invaded the area to form scrubby woodland interspersed with marshy swamps. The porous nature of the terrace means that rain quickly drains through the sandy soil, so that extensive watering has to be carried out during long, hot summers.

It is reasonable to ponder how the most famous botanic garden in the world should be sited on far-from-ideal soil. The answer is simply that the Gardens evolved quite fortuitously from the combination of two royal estates. At a time when transportation by water was widely used, the proximity of the river to both Richmond and Kew must have been a positive attraction to royalty. In 1721, several years before George II became king, he lived with the Princess of Wales at Ormonde Lodge (or Richmond Lodge) on the Richmond estate within the Old Deer Park which fronted on to the river. Several years after he succeeded to the throne in 1727, his son Frederick, Prince of Wales, took a lease of the adjacent Kew estate.

When he died in 1751, his widow Augusta, the Dowager Princess of Wales, appointed Sir William Chambers as her architectural adviser, but only six of his many buildings survive today: the Ruined Arch (1759); the Orangery (1760); the ten-storey Pagoda (1761–2); and the Temples of Bellona (1760), Aeolus (rebuilt in 1845) and Arethusa (1758).

Here also, a small arboretum and physic garden were laid out under the guidance of the Princess's horticultural adviser, Lord Bute. In 1761, he was responsible for acquiring several trees for Princess Augusta from the estate of his late uncle, the Duke of Argyll, at Whitton up the river near Hounslow. Among these trees, three still remain at Kew today: a locust tree or

LEFT: *Leafing out on the right of the picture is a ginkgo or maidenhair tree which was planted in Princess Augusta's garden in 1762. To the left is another plant native to China, an ancient wisteria, originally planted to grow up over the Great Stove glasshouse, but now festooning a gazebo.*

Maidenhair tree, Ginkgo biloba, *and* Wisteria sinensis
Arboretum
20 May 1991

false acacia, *Robinia pseudacacia*, a Japanese pagoda tree, *Sophora japonica*, and the largest maidenhair tree, *Ginkgo biloba*, in the Gardens.

After Princess Augusta's death in 1772, the two estates – Richmond and Kew – were united by her son George III. He appointed Joseph Banks (who travelled as naturalist on Captain Cook's *Endeavour* expedition to the Pacific) to advise on the botanical developments at Kew. It is estimated that some 7,000 specimens were introduced during George III's reign – mostly by Banks' collectors. Plants introduced during Banks' time included the Banksian rose, *Rosa banksiae*, a climber discovered at a Guangzhou nursery, south China, in 1807 by William Kerr; the tiger lily, *Lilium tigrinum*, with deep orange-red flowers bearing many purplish-black spots, and the cineraria, *Senecio cruentus*, from the Canaries, since bred into the many coloured forms now sold as pot plants.

Queen Charlotte, wife of George III, had her own menagerie near the Queen's Cottage where kangaroos, a blue nilgai from India and Algerian cows were kept until 1806. The surreal orange, blue and black bird of paradise flower, introduced to England from the Cape in 1773, was named *Strelitzia reginae* in honour of the Queen, formerly a princess of Mecklenburg-Strelitz.

The year 1820 saw the death of both King George III and Banks, after which the Gardens went into decline. Two decades later the ownership of Kew passed from the Crown to the State. Sir William Hooker was appointed the first official Director in 1841 of a modest 6 hectares (15 acres), but in the following five years, the area increased to over 100 hectares (250 acres). It was during Sir William's directorship that the Palm House (see p.46) was erected at a cost of £30,000 (equivalent to £1.2 million in 1992), and the Museums and Department of Economic Botany (1847), the Herbarium and Library (1852) came into being. When the Lake was excavated, the gravel was used to make a terrace for the Temperate House, the Main Block and two octagons being built during 1860–2, with the South and North Wings added several decades later to produce a glasshouse almost twice the area of the Palm House.

BELOW: *The South African crane flower, which was introduced to Kew by Sir Joseph Banks in 1773, was named in honour of George III's wife, Queen Charlotte, who was a Princess of Mecklenburg-Strelitz. The flowers, reminiscent of the African crowned crane, secrete nectar which attracts both sunbirds and sugarbirds. The weight of a landing bird causes the stamens to spring out and brush their pollen against its breast.*

Crane or bird-of-paradise flower, Strelitzia
  reginae
Temperate House
28 April 1991

The splendid vistas centred on the Palm House, extending north, south and west, which we now enjoy, were conceived in the 1840s by William Nesfield. From the Rose Garden adjacent to the Palm House, the Pagoda Vista unfolds to the south. No matter what the season, the Pagoda makes a spectacular focal point – even when its colours are not discernible, as it looms ghost-like from the autumnal mist. Instead of using a single tree species to line this avenue, over forty different kinds of trees were planted as opposite pairs. Running west from the edge of the Rose Garden is the Syon Vista, lined with evergreen Holm oaks, *Quercus ilex* – native to the Mediterranean region – interspersed with other trees. This vista runs right through the middle of the Gardens towards the Thames and Syon House across the river, although riverside plants now interrupt the view to the house. The Broad Walk, which stretches from a circular bed adjacent to the Pond up to the Orangery, is another of Nesfield's vistas, planted with cedars and tulip trees, *Liriodendron tulipifera*.

After Hooker's death, his son Joseph (later knighted) became Director in 1865 and made many additions to the Gardens. He planted the Pinetum, the Atlas cedars (1872), the Holly Walk (1874) and the Sweet Chestnut Avenue (1880) and created the Rock Garden in 1882. The buildings, on the other hand, were more modest than in his father's time, although the opening of the Jodrell Laboratory in 1876 was an important landmark from a scientific standpoint. It was T.J. Phillips Jodrell, a personal friend of Joseph Hooker, who financed the building and equipment of the laboratory for scientific research into the anatomy and physiology of plants. During the forty-four-year period when father and son Hooker between them directed Kew, they contributed greatly to the international reputation of the Gardens.

Within this century the Gardens have seen many changes. At the beginning of the Second World War, large lawns were ploughed up so that potatoes and other vegetables could be grown, while indoor tomatoes were produced in some of the glasshouses. A model allotment laid out as recommended by the Ministry of Agriculture and Fisheries to provide a family of four with vegetables virtually throughout the year, proved to be a great attraction to the public. When Chambers designed his ornate Pagoda for Kew, he could not have envisaged that it would be used during wartime for research into the velocity of bombs. Almost 50 metres (165 feet) high, the building had the floorboards cut away in each of its ten storeys, so that scientists could observe the way in which model bombs would fall from a height.

Notable additions to the Gardens in recent years include the pyramidal topped Alpine House (see p.105) opened in 1981 and, six years later, the Princess of Wales Conservatory, the glasshouse with the largest ground area at Kew. The futuristic design of the latter, with its low, extremely angular profile, is in complete contrast to that of the curvaceous Palm House. Built to replace twenty-six small houses, the prime concern was to conserve energy. Most of the space is below ground level and there are no side walls. It is divided into ten distinct environmental zones, in each of which the temperature, humidity, ventilation and lighting are precisely controlled by computer. Every two minutes the conditions in each zone are checked and, if necessary, adjustments are made. Here, optimum growing conditions are provided for plants from habitats as diverse as arid deserts, humid tropics, mangrove swamps and tropical freshwaters.

Kew's fortunes certainly waxed and waned in 1987 for, not long after the excitement associated with the opening of the Princess of Wales Conservatory had subsided, the Gardens were buffeted by a storm of near hurricane force

ABOVE: *Within the Ornamental section of the Princess of Wales Conservatory, two quite distinct kinds of* Impatiens *can be seen. The large-flowered New Guinea hybrids – with green, red or bronze foliage, often variegated, and white, pink, salmon or red flowers – are becoming increasingly popular as pot plants. But the metre-high* Impatiens niamniamensis *from Bioko, an island off the coast of Cameroon, bears spectacularly coloured flowers, each resembling a miniature parrot with a green hood attached to a red spur by a yellow tube.*

Impatiens niamniamensis
Princess of Wales Conservatory, Ornamental section
2 August 1991

RIGHT: *The hot and humid atmosphere provided within the Wet Tropics section of the Princess of Wales Conservatory allows tropical rainforest plants to flourish. The large leaves belong to a perennial giant herb known as elephant's ear, which frequents humid lowland forests in tropical Asia. The plant below, with white bract-like spathes, belongs to the same family, the Araceae, but originates in South America.*

Elephant's ear, Colocasia indica *with* Spathiphyllum wallisii
Princess of Wales Conservatory, Wet Tropics section
10 May 1991

during the night of 15–16 October 1987. Overnight 10 per cent of Kew's 9,000 trees were felled or severely damaged – as many as might be expected to be lost by natural causes over a fifteen-year period. Among the notable losses was a specimen of the original introduction to cultivation of the Caucasian elm, *Zelkova carpinifolia* (1762), the very rare elm *Ulnus villosa*, and a 200-year-old Turkey oak, *Quercus cerris*, near the Palm House Pond. The Gardens had to be closed for ten days while some of the paths and roads were cleared. Seeing the Gardens on the day after the storm, I found that the most striking change was the temporary loss of vistas on this flat site, as huge leafy crowns (most of the felled trees were deciduous) interrupted the views created by landscape designers during the last century. The sudden loss of so many trees at Kew caught the attention of the world's press and media. Less well publicized, however, was the gradual, but none the less heavy, loss of some 600 trees during 1976 and 1977, triggered by the severe drought of 1976 combined with the prevalence of Dutch elm and sooty bark diseases.

The effect of the 1987 losses at Kew, however, was not entirely negative. For one thing, the gaps so created enabled a wider representation of species to be planted within some collections. Scientists working on tree roots in the Jodrell Laboratory suddenly had a quantity of material – and a range of species – beyond their wildest dreams. Exposed root systems were measured and systematically photographed. Because the precise ages of many wind-blown trees were known, sections of trunks could be used both to research the ageing of trees and to look for indications of the effects of air pollution, including acid rain.

In collaboration with Task Force Trees of the Countryside Commission, Kew scientists analysed completed questionnaires about windblown trees in south-east England. This work provided information on how tree roots develop in different soils and locations, as well as on the instability of certain species in high winds, which will be invaluable not only to landscape gardeners but also to urban planners. Much of the windblown timber from the storm was sold; some, however, was donated to craftsmen. They had the rare opportunity of working unusual woods to create unique pieces of furniture, some of which were exhibited at Kew.

Not long after all the additional work associated with the October 1987 storm had been completed, more storms in January 1990 felled, or damaged beyond repair, a further 120 trees at Kew. On this occasion, it was mostly broad-leaved evergreens or conifers that suffered, rather than the deciduous trees which had shed all their leaves by this time of year.

Later in 1990 the Gardens opened yet another innovative major building to the public. Like the Princess of Wales Conservatory, this – the Sir Joseph Banks Building – also had to save energy. Both the temperature and humidity inside had to remain constant, for it was to house reference plants and many rare books, as well as an extensive collection of artefacts made from plants. Another stipulation was that the building should not impinge on the view of Kew Palace – a Grade I listed building – from Kew Bridge. In a major architectural competition which attracted over 270 entries, the winning design was by Manning Clamp and Partners, whose solution to the various requirements was to create a building extending well below ground and to cover it with earth banks – the first public building to utilize earth-shelter insulation in Britain. As the banks are now well vegetated, the building blends in well with its surroundings; yet the area of exposed glass exterior appears larger to the eye when it is repeated as a reflection in the adjacent lake.

ABOVE: *The buds of many rhododendron flowers appear as a darker hue than the fully open flowers.* Rhododendron manglesii *has deep pink buds which open into pale pink flowers.*

Rhododendron manglesii
Rhododendron Dell
13 May 1992

BELOW: *A variety of temperate forest plants – perennials, climbers and shrubs as well as trees – is grown in the Woodland Garden. This area is particularly attractive in late spring and early summer when the rhododendrons and* Mecanopsis *are in flower.*

Rhododendrons beneath trees
Woodland Garden
13 May 1992

Named after the Garden's first unofficial director, the building is now Kew's Centre for Economic Botany. The first exhibition here, an audio-visual display entitled 'The Thread of Life', opened in 1990. Depicting the multifarious uses of cellulose, which is obtained from plants – most simply ropes, cane and rattan furniture, cotton and linen – it showed how, once it was discovered that this substance could be altered, the potential for cellulose-derived products seemed almost endless. For example, the celluloid backing for photographic films (as used to take the pictures in this book), acetates and textile fibres such as viscose all come from cellulose. Indeed, the discovery of how viscose fibres could be produced from wood had been made in the Jodrell Laboratory at Kew at the turn of the century.

If the cultivation of fast-growing plants is managed carefully, cellulose can be produced time and time again from the same piece of land. In other words unlike oil it is a renewable resource. Energy derived from plants – from burning wood, charcoal, plant residues or animal dung (a by-product of plants) is known as biomass energy or bioenergy. It is not a new idea; after all, we have been burning wood for thousands of years. Our fuel of the future may even be derived from bacteria breaking down cellulose products to produce biogas, a mixture of methane and carbon dioxide. In fact, production of biogas is already a commercial operation in several parts of the world. Animal dung is used to fuel biogas plants in China (from pigs) and in India (from cattle), producing compost for farmers and biogas to power electricity generators. The discovery that water hyacinth, *Eichhornia crassipes*, which can be seen floating on pools in the Princess of Wales Conservatory, is a potential biogas producer, makes it doubly attractive. Although this tropical aquatic plant is a pest in many countries, because it grows so rapidly and soon chokes waterways, it is effective in removing nitrates from the water. It can be costly to remove plants from waterways and dump them on land, but if they are fermented and used for biogas production, the operation could well prove to be profitable. More information about plants and our dependence on them can be found throughout the Gardens and within the Victoria Gate Visitor Centre.

Kew is very much a garden for all seasons; long after flowers have faded and herbaceous plants died down, there is always something of interest in the glasshouses, as well as the specimen trees throughout the grounds. Briefly, late winter to early spring is a time when witch hazels, *Hamamelis* spp. and mahonias flower; the first bulbs, as well as frost and snow-resistent perennials such as Christmas roses, appear. Snowdrops, followed by wild daffodils, carpet the ground beneath the pleached hornbeam alley in the Queen's Garden. But the most spectacular bulb show, in terms of sheer numbers, has to be the crocus carpets planted in 1987 on either side of the path which leads from Victoria Gate to King William's Temple. Depending on the weather, the peak time for this display may be in the latter part of February (as in 1990) or well into March (as in 1991). Spring is also the season for magnolias,

camellias, forsythias, flowering cherries and lilacs, as well as the spring bedding displays.

May – when the native deciduous trees leaf out and azure drifts of bluebells enrich the Queen's Cottage Grounds – is a glorious month at Kew, as it is in almost any garden in southern Britain. It is also the best time to see the Rhododendron Dell, as well as the Laburnum Tunnel in the Queen's Garden. Wisterias are in flower then too, and an old gnarled specimen of *Wisteria sinensis* is worthy of mention. Now growing over a gazebo, beside one of the oldest trees at Kew – a maidenhair tree – it once covered the east end of the Great Stove glasshouse, built in 1761 and dismantled in 1861. The Great Stove was used for growing delicate plants which flourished in the humid heat created by the fermentation of pieces of oak bark (a by-product of the tanning industry) packed into a bed in the centre of the glasshouse.

By midsummer the Rose Garden, the Grass Garden, the Queen's Garden and the summer bedding displays are at their peak. During Victorian times bedding displays, including carpet bedding, were popular in gardens throughout Britain. Nowadays such labour intensive displays are much reduced at Kew, although the beds which line the Broad Walk and the bi-coloured formal parterre in front of the Palm House are changed twice a year. After Canada geese damaged the Palm House beds in both 1986 and 1987 (when they devoured the lobelias and trod on the busy lizzies) a low fence had to be erected around the beds.

Walking through the central transept of the Palm House from the Pond entrance out through the opposite doors leads to the formal Rose Garden and the extensive Syon Vista beyond. Both old and new varieties of cluster

ABOVE: *Red and white were the colours chosen for the 1991 spring bedding displays along the Broad Walk. It was not until one month after this photograph was taken that the tulips at the north end of this long vista opened.*

Tulipa 'Stockholm' with double daisies,
  Bellis 'Pomponnette white'
Broad Walk
12 April 1991

RIGHT: *As winter gives way to spring, one of the main attractions at Kew are the crocus carpets on either side of the path leading from Victoria Gate to King William's Temple. Planting of the 1.6 million crocus corms – a gift from the Reader's Digest to represent their 1987 UK circulation – was done by cutting and rolling back the turf.*

Crocus vernus *hybrids*
View looking towards Temple of Arethusa
23 February 1990

LEFT: *Beyond the southern end of the Palm House beds set in lawns are planted to illustrate the historical development of garden roses. Here can be seen a particularly striking China rose which produces a succession of single flowers that first appear the colour of chamois leather and change with age to pale pink and finally to a deep cerise.*

Rosa chinensis mutabilis
History of Garden Roses display
13 June 1989

(floribunda) and large-flowered (hybrid tea) roses are grown in the main semi-circular garden, while the ancestry of modern roses is explained on display panels in beds of old roses planted in an area to the south. In autumn, many of these old roses develop attractive hips.

Summer is also the prime time for the Order Beds in the Herbaceous Ground, which was a walled kitchen garden when Kew was a royal estate. A design for a parterre in this area, made by Decimus Burton in 1847, was passed over in favour of regular rectangular beds. Here a huge concentration of annual and perennial dicotyledonous plants from temperate latitudes, and some tropical annuals, are grown. As was the custom in old physic gardens, the plants are arranged systematically, with those from one family sharing one or more beds. Thus plants from the mallow family (Malvaceae) will be found in adjacent beds. This aids the appreciation of the botanical relationships of plants and how they have come to be classified into distinct families and genera within the families.

Anyone who is familiar with British wild flowers will recognize many widespread, as well as rarer, species growing in the Order Beds; plants such as sea campion, soapwort, deadly nightshade, silverweed and cornflower, to name but a few, share beds with relatives from Europe and North America.

In late summer the Compositae (daisy family) beds are worth looking at for the pink stems and flower clusters of dodder, *Cuscuta* – a plant that lives as a parasite. Because dodder lacks green chlorophyll, it is unable to manufacture starches and sugars; instead it lives as a parasite on green plants. Britain's two wild species of dodder normally parasitize stinging nettle, hop, gorse and ling, *Calluna vulgaris*, but at Kew dodder grows well on a variety of composites from Europe, Japan and Asia.

Dodder can invade cultivated areas via seeds in topsoil or in mud carried on the soles of shoes. Belonging to the convolvulus family, dodder plants have thin pink (or sometimes yellow) stems that entwine around the host plant.

RIGHT: *The plants in the formal parterre outside the Palm House are changed twice a year; the spring bedding is planted out in October and the summer bedding in late May or early June. The two-colour scheme for this 1991 summer planting was pink and silver.*

Pink and silver colour scheme of summer bedding
Outside the Palm House
29 September 1991

Where the dodder stem makes contact with the host stem, it produces peg-like structures that penetrate inside so the host's food supply can be tapped. Broomrapes are another group of parasitic plants which also appear in the Order Beds at Kew, while ivy broomrape grows on ivy outside the School of Horticulture building.

As the day length shortens with the onset of autumn, so tree fruits ripen and leaves of deciduous trees begin to change colour. Much of the planting around the Banks Pond is especially attractive in late autumn. Most conspicuously there is an extensive stand of sea buckthorn, *Hippophaë rhamnoides*, bearing clusters of orange fruits atop the silvery-grey foliage. Nearby, a display of the Chinese shrub, *Callicarpa bodnieri* var. *giraldii*, carries spectacular purple fruits on bare twigs. There are also plantings of British shrubs noted for their colourful fruits; the guelder rose, *Viburnum opulus*, and dog rose, *Rosa canina*. In the Temperate House the Cape heaths and proteas begin to flower, while the Heather Garden is worth a visit at this time of year and on throughout the winter. On either side of the path leading to the Ice House, on the west side of the Princess of Wales Conservatory, is an interesting area planted with winter-flowering shrubs and plants with colourful barks. Indeed, winter is the best time to appreciate the varied colours and texture to be found among barks of both broadleaved and coniferous trees.

The Australian House should not be missed in December and January, when the air is heavy with the scent of flowering acacias. These bring welcome colour at a time of year when the grounds are lacking their floriferous displays and the birds have stripped most of the fruit from the trees.

Today, the Living Collections and the grounds are maintained by about 180 full-time staff assisted by the students (see p.146). Horses were used to pull carts and wagons at Kew as recently as the 1950s, when they were replaced by tractors. Now 100 hectares (40 acres) of grassland, including lawns, are mown by 28 small machines and four large ride-on machines while a mobile hydraulic lift is used for planting epiphytic plants on artificial trees and for pruning plants extending high into the glasshouse interiors.

In recent years, Kew staff have been looking at a variety of renewable composting materials, including straw and leaves. Bark is used in some places and much larger quantities of waste plant matter from the Gardens are now being composted. Until quite recently natural peat was used extensively both outside and for potting compost. Now Kew is setting an example to help reduce the destruction of Britain's natural peat deposits by using a 100 per cent renewable peat substitute, made from coconut husks, for propagating nearly all plants. Over a long period of time lowland peat deposits have gradually been lost to agriculture, but during the last three decades, extraction of peat for the horticultural trade has been the major threat. A growing concern about these unique habitats has provided the impetus to find peat substitutes for horticultural purposes. Coir fibre pith is a by-product of the waste from coconut husks in Sri Lanka. This peat substitute has the advantage of a faster rewetting time and a better water-holding capacity than traditional peat and, in trials done at Kew, fuchsias were found to grow better and to produce more flowers in coir-based potting compost than in a peat one.

In fact, the use of coir at Kew is not a recent innovation, for coconut husks loaded as ballast in ships from Kingston, Jamaica, were used at Kew in 1762 in the Stove House. Then, when it was realized that peat was just as good and did not have to be imported, it was used thereafter. Now, more than two centuries later, coir is back in favour again.

RIGHT: *The fiery red flowers, tinged with yellow, of this leguminous shrub grace many a garden in both the Old and New World tropics. Delicate pinnate mimosa-like leaves belie the prickly branches beneath.*

Barbados pride, Caesalpinia pulcherrima
Palm House
5 September 1991

BELOW: *By midsummer, several plants in the compositae beds in the Herbaceous Ground will be seen to have pink threads twining around them. These are the stems of dodder, a parasitic plant without roots and leaves, which germinates only after the host plant is well established. Completely lacking chlorophyll, dodder is dependent on tapping the food supply of its host, ultimately producing small clusters of pale pink flowers.*

Parasitic dodder, Cuscuta sp., *on* Artemisia borealis
Compositae beds in the Herbaceous Ground
14 August 1991

Kew is also setting an example by using biological, in preference to chemical, means to control pests in the glasshouses. Biological control became a necessity at Kew when scientists working in the Jodrell Laboratory realized that pesticide residues might affect their experiments. Several years later, biological control was introduced to all the Kew glasshouses open to the public. Natural parasites and predators of pest species are released from small packets which may be seen hanging on some plants. Examples include two kinds of parasitic wasp – *Encarsia formosa*, which attacks glasshouse whitefly scales and turns them black and *Aphidius matricariae*, which attacks aphids. Bacterial and fungal diseases of aphids and caterpillars are now also used as a means of biological control.

LEFT: *Sea buckthorn naturally frequents coastal regions where it is often wind-pruned, but a vigorous, tall stand can be seen at Kew beside the Banks Pond. As the shrub produces inconspicuous flowers, it is grown for its bright orange fruits which are wind-resistant and crowd the upper branches in autumn among the narrow silvery leaves.*

Sea buckthorn, Hippophäe rhamnoides
Beside Banks Pond
28 December 1991

LEFT: *During the latter part of October and the early part of November, the Gardens are transformed as the leaves of deciduous trees turn a riot of reds, oranges, golds, yellows and browns before they fall. Here, cherry leaves add a splash of colour, complemented by the yellowing leaves of an Indian bean tree and the sombre evergreen needles of a conifer behind. In spring, this Japanese cherry produces very pale pink flowers that smell faintly of almonds.*

Yoshino cherry, Prunus x yedoensis, *with Indian bean tree,* Catalpa bignonioides
Arboretum
30 October 1991

RIGHT: *Beside a path winding through the Rock Garden, there is a striking deciduous Japanese maple with finely dissected purple leaves. After the clusters of small reddish flowers appear, winged fruits begin to develop.*

Japanese maple, Acer palmatum 'Dissectum Atropurpureum'
Rock Garden
15 October 1990

Larger natural predators have also been introduced to the glasshouses, including Chinese painted quail in the Science Support houses and reptiles in the Palm House. A shipment of lizards and geckos, illegally imported to Britain early in 1992, was saved from an untimely end when Customs and Excise decided to hand them over to Kew Gardens.

Over the years, the fortunes of The Royal Botanic Gardens, Kew, may have waxed and waned; but it could be argued that now, more than at any time during Kew's history, they are poised to play their most demanding role yet. The research being carried out there, as well as the varied educational programmes, will not only have far-reaching effects for mankind in general, but also cannot fail to increase our appreciation of plants.

CHAPTER TWO

TEMPERATE FOREST PLANTS

*Temperate forests occur in both the northern
and the southern hemispheres and
comprise both evergreen as well as deciduous
types. The latter are especially attractive
when they develop spectacular colours in
autumn, and since the forest floor is
well lit after the leaves have fallen, it is
enlivened with carpets of wild
flowers in spring.*

UNLIKE PLANTS of tropical forests, which have to be cosseted under glass at Kew, hardy temperate forest plants occur outside all over the Gardens, though some more tender ones are grown in the Temperate and Australian Houses. Mature temperate trees are especially important components in the landscaping of the Gardens. Over the centuries trees have been planted in the grounds so that they both satisfy the aesthetic eye and allow botanists readily to locate a specimen.

Nowadays rainforest destruction is constantly in the news, deplored by so many inhabitants of temperate countries; yet large areas of their native forests have also been destroyed by man – in many cases so long ago that there is no trace of the original forest. Most of the British landscape we know today has been shaped by the hand of man over a very long period. At one time forests covered some 60 per cent of the land surface in Britain; after the end of the Second World War this figure had dwindled to a mere 5 per

LEFT: *A mixed temperate forest in North Carolina displays
a rich array of colours in October as the deciduous trees
develop their autumnal hues among evergreen conifers.
In calm weather, the colours linger; an overnight gale, however,
will strip away the leaves to reveal the bare
winter branches.*

cent. Since the Forestry Commission came into being in 1919, however, the figure has gradually increased: by 1991 it had doubled to 10 per cent; and now, for every tree felled, it is estimated that three young trees are planted. Compared to deciduous forests, coniferous monocultures, which make up the vast majority of Forestry Commission planting, support a very limited range of flora and fauna; but in recent years, some mixed woodlands, so much more attractive to wildlife, have been planted.

From archaeological evidence we know that forest clearance began in Britain around 2500 BC. Forests were cleared not only to provide agricultural land for grazing and growing crops, but also to produce timber for building and to use as firewood. In medieval times, efforts were made to manage woodlands so that timber for fencing and firewood could be renewed. Coppicing (the practice of cutting certain deciduous trees down to ground level, so that they produce multiple stems) had been tried before without much success because stock munched the succulent new shoots. However, the problem was solved when a 1483 statute authorized recently coppiced woods to be enclosed for seven years. Pollarding (the practice of lopping a deciduous tree some 2 metres ($6\frac{1}{2}$ feet) above the ground so that it produces many branches) was a way in which renewable timber could be produced without the need to fence out grazing animals. Some examples of old pollarded trees can still be seen today in Hampshire's New Forest, Burnham Beeches in Buckinghamshire and Epping Forest in Essex.

As populations have grown within temperate regions, so the need for agricultural land has increased and natural forests have been felled. In a comparatively recently settled country, such as New Zealand, the loss of indigenous forest has occurred within a short time span. More than 80 per cent of New Zealand was once covered by native forest, which has been cleared at such a rate over the last 150 years that only one third now remains. In recent years, temperate forests (especially coniferous forests in northern Europe) have been killed by acid rain, the end product of industrial emissions that are carried up into the atmosphere.

Temperate trees are so much part of the Kew scene that to list them all would result in a catalogue of scientific names. In the northern part of the Arboretum (which includes the original 1759 botanic garden), trees are planted in mixed decorative groups. Elsewhere, they are arranged by genera; thus *Fagus* (beech), *Fraxinus* (ash) and *Quercus* (oak) are grouped in distinct areas, not unlike the way in which herbaceous plants are grouped according to their family in the Order Beds. Here are trees from both northern and southern temperate zones, from Europe, North America, China, Japan, Australia and New Zealand. Among the *Fagus* collection are *F. engleriana* from central China, and several cultivars of the European beech, *Fagus sylvatica*, including *F.s.* 'Grandidentata' (with coarsely-toothed leaves), the erect Dawyck beech, *F.s.* 'Dawyck', and a weeping beech, *F.s.* 'Pendula', with branches drooping down to the ground. (These have had to be propped up on one side of the tree to allow a clear passage along the path.) An even larger weeping beech can be seen on the east side of the Broad Walk. Once the leaves have fallen, the ramifications of the branches become apparent. Many cascade down to the ground only to turn up again, looking not unlike a gigantic spider on the move.

Mention has already been made of the tree-lined vistas that greatly add to the enjoyment of visiting the Gardens. At the north end of the Arboretum, isolated large specimen trees set in lawns include an oriental plane, *Plantanus orientalis*, and a fine chestnut-leaved oak, *Quercus castaneifolia*. Here their lower branches can develop to the full, because they are not crowded out by close neighbours as would be the case in a natural forest.

Temperate forests, although not so species-rich as tropical rainforests, none the less contain a mix of plants ranging from mature trees, shrubs, climbers and herbaceous plants to mosses and lichens living as epiphytes on trunks and branches, as well as fungi. Most cap fungi which appear among leaf litter or on lawns are harmless enough to plants, but huge clumps of honey fungus, *Armillaria mellea*, are proof that lethal, black bootlace threads are attacking live trees. Some bracket fungi will also attack living trees, entering via crotches which begin to rot from semi-permanent miniature pools. One of the glories of deciduous (as compared with coniferous) forests is the carpets of wild flowers which appear each spring. By comparison, the interior of a regimented coniferous plantation is so dark that few green plants are able to grow, apart from along rides and in clearings.

BELOW: *The appearance of temperate trees can change quite dramatically from one season to another. When the red oak from eastern North America begins to leaf out in spring, it is flushed with acid yellow; after a few weeks, the leaves become dull green until they turn yellow and brown in autumn. This tree, which was planted at Kew in 1874, is one of a fine collection of oaks along the western side of the Gardens.*

Red oak, Quercus rubra, *with Canada geese,* Branta canadensis
Near Riverside Avenue
7 May 1991

RIGHT: *The arrangement of leaves on branches – known as the leaf mosaic – is best appreciated in newly opened leaves before they are damaged by herbivorous insects. Here, new beech leaves appear to glow when viewed against a sunlit sky.*

RIGHT: *The arrangement of leaves on branches – known as the leaf mosaic – is best appreciated in newly opened leaves before they are damaged by herbivorous insects. Here, new beech leaves appear to glow when viewed against a sunlit sky.*

Leaves of the beech, Fagus sylvatica
Arboretum
12 May 1991

LEFT: *Kew has many exotic and rare plants, but one of the glories of the Gardens is the azure carpet of native bluebells which transform the Queen's Cottage grounds in spring. In hot weather, the spectacle lasts for only a few days. Bluebells occur throughout Britain in hedgerows and deciduous woods but, since they need light to flourish, they do particularly well in grounds with scattered trees and in coppiced woodlands.*

Bluebells, Hyacinthoides non-scripta
Queen's Cottage grounds
9 May 1991

It may come as a surprise to learn that one of the finest semi-natural bluebell woods in the London region is tucked away in the south-west corner of Kew Gardens. The Queen's Cottage Grounds was the last major area to be added to the Gardens, and now contains some large native beech trees, within its 16 hectares (40 acres). Since Kew acquired this area, trees and shrubs native to Britain have been replanted here. With the exception of bluebell time, this part of the Gardens attracts few visitors apart from keen birdwatchers. But many other wild flowers of British woodlands occur here too, albeit not in such abundance as the bluebells. The tall stems of rosebay willowherb may be conspicuous enough, but more effort will be needed to locate spikes of the spectacular martagon lily, *Lilium martagon,* a doubtful British native.

Beech trees look their best early in May, when they are clothed in a pale green as they leaf out, and again in late October or early November, when they turn striking shades of yellow, gold and brown. The transformation of deciduous trees in general from their drab green summer cloak to their

RIGHT: *Clumps of single-flowered lesser celandine are widespread throughout Britain in woods and along stream banks. This picture shows the uncommon, but attractive, double form which also flowers in spring.*

Double lesser celandine, Ranunculus ficaria
'Flore Pleno'
Woodland Garden
12 April 1991

LEFT: *It is curious that such a prickly shrub as butcher's broom, which frequents dry woods among rocks, should belong to the lily family. Green, star-shaped, female flowers arise in the centre of the leaf-like stems known as cladodes. Throughout winter, red marble-sized fruits persist. The shrub's common name originates from the old custom of butchers decorating their Christmas sirloins with berried twigs.*

Butcher's broom, Ruscus aculeatus
Bed with Arbutus *trees, north-west of King William's Temple*
22 January 1991

autumn mantle, varies not only from one species to another, but also according to the location of individual trees. This is clearly borne out by looking at individual tulip trees in the Gardens along the Broad Walk and in the Azalea Garden. The effect of aspect can be seen by comparing the rate of colour change in the pair of tulip trees at the end of the Broad Walk: the one nearest the Palm House turns first. Even parts of the same tree can show a marked difference, with south-facing branches turning before north-facing ones. The best colours develop when freezing nights alternate with sunny days and, because colour change is a prelude to leaf fall, the colours will persist only if the air is still. Among the trees which consistently produce spectacular autumn hues at Kew are a specimen of chittamwood, *Cotinus obovatus*, beside the path between Victoria Gate and the Temple of Bellona and a *Parrotia persica* in the Duke's Garden.

Leaves and stems get their green colour from the pigment chlorophyll which is essential for photosynthesis, the process whereby green plants produce carbohydrates from carbon dioxide and water. Most plants photosynthesize via their leaves, but some have flattened leaf-like stems, or cladodes, functioning in the same way as leaves. Butcher's broom, *Ruscus aculeatus*, a plant of dry European woodlands, is a good example: extensive clumps with red spherical fruits attached to the centre of the spiny-tipped cladodes can be seen at Kew in winter in a bed with strawberry trees, *Arbutus* spp., to the west of King William's Temple and to the west of the Banks Pond.

As the daylight hours dramatically shorten during the onset of autumn, chlorophyll is no longer produced in leaves of deciduous trees and the colour of the orange carotenoid and yellow xanthophyll pigments (which were previously masked by chlorophyll) begins to show. The brilliant yellow coloration of trees such as birches and the maidenhair tree are formed by the disintegration of green chlorophyll; while the vibrant reds of sumachs, some acers and North American oaks are formed by anthocyanin pigments forming in the cell sap.

All trees shed their leaves but, unlike deciduous species which lose theirs over a matter of days, evergreens constantly shed a few throughout the year. Apart from a few leaves or needles on the ground, leaf loss is not apparent on

RIGHT: *Although widespread in Europe, this arum is not nearly as common in Britain as cuckoo pint. It is confined to a narrow band near the sea along the south coast. By December, the leaves are well developed, but by the time the colourful fruiting spikes develop in late summer the following year, they have died down completely. In 1840, the herbalist Parkinson recommended the powdered dried root of the arum taken with sugar as a cure for drunkenness.*

Fruit of Italian arum, Arum italicum
*Bed near rotunda on mount, Queen's Garden
27 August 1991*

trees such as hollies or pines. When deciduous trees are fully leafed out, they lose water vapour via evaporation through microscopic pores, called stomata, in the leaf surface. A mature oak, for example, can lose more than 150 litres (33 gallons) of water on a summer's day. The passage of water via the roots up the stems to the leaves ensures that mineral salts are taken up from the soil. Shrubs and herbaceous plants also lose water in the same way and here wilting – caused when the rate of water loss exceeds the rate of uptake – is more obvious than in large trees.

When the ground becomes frozen in winter, water cannot be taken up by tree roots to replace the loss through evaporation, so deciduous trees shed their leaves before the onset of winter as a precaution against this. Evergreen temperate trees have overcome this problem by reducing the rate at which they lose water. Typically they have a thick, waxy coating to the leaf (such as holly) or needle-like inrolled leaves, as seen in pines.

As early as Victorian times, smogs caused problems at Kew. Glass in the houses was so badly covered with grime from smogs that the light transmission was much reduced. The sooty layer deposited on the leaves of evergreen trees and needles of conifers decreased the amount of light reaching inside the leaf, which made photosynthesis less efficient and reduced the growth rate. By the 1920s there was a pressing need to find a site with cleaner air for the cultivation of conifers. Bedgebury in Kent was selected for the National Pinetum which was set up as a joint project between Kew and the Forestry Commission during 1924–5. Since London became a smokeless zone, all evergreens at Kew have become noticeably healthier.

While the majority of trees which turn colour at Kew are broad-leaved, some conifers with soft needles also change colour and shed all their leaves at once. Needles of the European larch, *Larix decidua*, turn yellow in autumn, while the rich gold colour of golden larch, *Pseudolarix amabilis*, from China, can be seen near the Waterlily Pond. The swamp cypress, *Taxodium distichum*, from the south-east flood plains of the United States, turns a foxy-brown

BELOW: *The colour and texture of bark show up most clearly on deciduous trees after the leaves have dropped. The grooves on sweet chestnut bark develop a distinct spiral growth in old trees as shown in this specimen, one of several along Chestnut Avenue running parallel to and north of the Lake.*

Bark of the sweet chestnut, Castanea sativa
Chestnut Avenue
31 March 1992

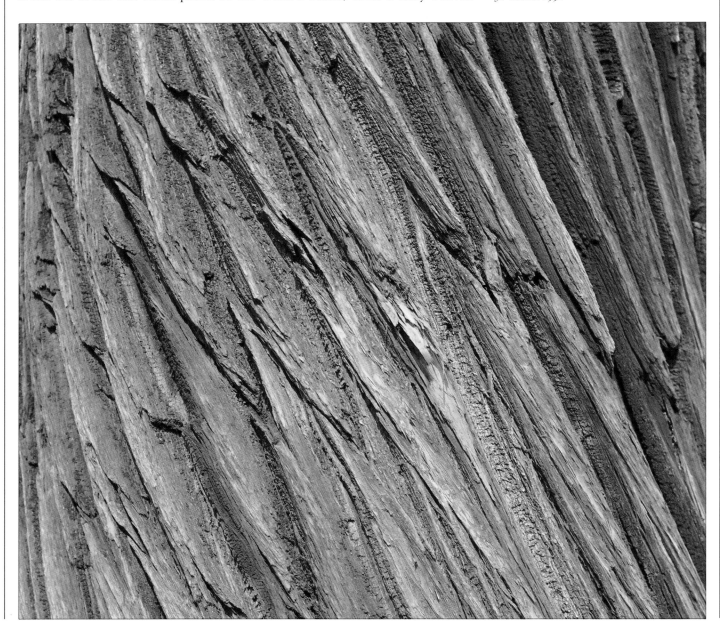

ABOVE: *Native to North America, from Nova Scotia down as far as Florida, the tulip tree was one of the first trees to be introduced to Britain from that part of the world. The distinctively shaped leaves, with their straight-edged apex, turn golden yellow in autumn before they fall.*

Fallen leaves of tulip tree, Liriodendron tulipifera
Azalea Garden
30 October 1991

colour, often quite late in November; there are several in the Gardens, including one to the west of the Rose Garden and one beside the Waterlily Pond adjacent to a dawn redwood, *Metasequoia glyptostroboides*. The dawn redwood, which was discovered in south-east China as recently as 1941 and introduced to Britain in 1947, is a living relic of a genus previously known only as fossil forms. The feathery leaves of this tree are equally attractive in spring, when they leaf out as a bright, fresh green, and in autumn, when they turn a pinky-brown colour.

After leaf fall, winter is the time when the branching pattern and the colour and texture of the bark can be best appreciated. Close to the decorative display entrance of the Princess of Wales Conservatory is *Acer griseum*, with its flaking bark; west of King William's Temple is the flaking bark of *Stuartia pseudocamellia* and the russet bark (greatly enriched by rain) of several kinds of strawberry tree, including *Arbutus unedo*, which grows well in woods around the Killarney Lakes in Ireland. Other trees noted for their bark are the snakebark maples growing near the Marianne North Gallery and many of the eucalyptus or gum trees from Australia. A few eucalyptus trees, with their typical flaking bark, are planted in the lawn around the Aquatic Garden, while a larger collection can be seen near the temporary cycad house. Sharing the North Octagon of the Temperate House with many New Zealand plants is *Eucalyptus coccifera* from Tasmania, with its attractive cascading whitebarked branches.

The bark of the outsized sweet or Spanish chestnuts, *Castanea sativa*, which can be seen in the Chestnut Avenue running parallel to Syon Vista, is infinitely more interesting than the smooth bark of young trees. Gradually vertical cracks develop, until finally deep ridges spiral around the dark brown trunk, producing a distinctively sculptured bole.

Winter is also a good time for studying the bark of evergreen conifers, since the sun then follows a much lower arc, lighting the trunks more obliquely. One of the most decorative of all conifers must be the Chinese lacebark pine, *Pinus bungeana*, which peels off bits at a time to produce a patchwork of pink, green and cream areas. Named after Alexander von Bunge, who discovered it growing in a Buddhist temple garden near Beijing in 1831, this pine was introduced to Britain by Robert Fortune in 1846. A pair of trees grow at Kew, east of the Waterlily House, and there are others in the Pinetum near the Lake.

Two of Kew's oldest trees are a locust tree or false acacia, and a maidenhair or ginkgo, both planted in 1762 in the first botanic garden initiated at Kew by Princess Augusta. The locust tree, approaching the end of its natural lifespan, certainly looks its age with several metal bands encircling the decaying trunk. The ginkgo, on the other hand, still has many years to go before it reaches the reputed great age of some specimens planted around Buddhist temples in the Far East, where it is regarded as a sacred tree. Belonging to an ancient plant group which flourished some 200 million years ago, at a time when dinosaurs roamed the earth, it has curious fan-shaped deciduous leaves resembling those of a maidenhair fern.

As the male and female flowers are produced on separate trees, both kinds of ginkgo must be planted in close proximity for the oval, yellow fruits to be produced – although some people might argue that it is better to avoid producing the fruits with their evil-smelling fleshy coats. Ginkgos are often planted as street trees in Japan, where care is taken to plant only male trees; but the nut inside the fruit, when roasted, is considered a delicacy in both Japan and China. The large Kew tree is male and, after a female branch was successfully grafted in 1911, it bore fruit until, it is reputed, the branch was inadvertently pruned! There is a female tree in the nursery border near the Tea Bar and, close to the original ginkgo, young specimens have been planted. These have not yet flowered so their sex is unknown.

Another tree dating from the original botanic garden is a Japanese pagoda tree, which grows near the Princess of Wales Conservatory. Planted in 1761 it is long past its best and, having developed a prostrate habit, it has to be propped up in several places. Because it was suffering some decay, part of the main trunk was infilled by tree surgeons and, where a crack developed between the filling and the trunk, a pair of blue tits managed to squeeze through to make their nest inside. The specific name, *japonica*, is a misnomer since the tree is a native of China, not Japan. Pagoda trees can be seen in courtyards and parks, as well as lining roads, in Chinese cities. The panicles of leguminous creamish-white flowers are produced in September – long after most trees have flowered in Britain. In China the flowers are used for dying cloth yellow or for changing blue cloth to a green colour.

Almost opposite an aged stone pine, *Pinus pinea* (planted in 1846 and also supported by props) is another *Sophora* from China, *S. davidii*, which bears small blue and white flowers in June. But a member of this genus which no visitor can miss when it flowers in May is *S. microphylla*, collected by Banks from New Zealand in 1772. An example outside the walled Duke's Garden, beside the path leading to the Alpine House, produces a spectacular show of yellow flowers in May.

Tree leaves come in all shapes and sizes. They can be a simple, single blade with triangular (silver birch, *Betula pendula*), heart (Judas tree, *Cercis siliquastrum*) or palmate (sycamore, *Acer pseudoplatanus*) shapes, or they can be a compound leaf made of several small leaflets (false acacia). It is the shape of the

ABOVE: *The larch of the European alps was first introduced to the British Isles around 1629. It is a graceful, deciduous conifer, producing fresh green needles each spring which turn golden yellow in autumn. Before the new needles show, erect pink cones – often referred to as 'roses' – appear on the same tree as the yellow male button flowers. After pollination, the cones gradually become woody.*

Female flowers of European larch, Larix decidua
Arboretum
31 March 1992

leaves and their arrangement in relation to one another that gives rise to the distinctive leaf mosaic for each species. This can be seen most easily by viewing a branch against the sky immediately after the leaves have opened out in spring. For a leaf to receive the maximum amount of sunlight, it should not overlap with its neighbours.

If flowering plants are to produce seeds, they must first be pollinated. Coniferous trees, such as larches, pines, firs, spruces, hemlocks, cypresses and the Sierra redwood, *Sequoiadendron giganteum*, are wind-pollinated. Since they do not have to attract animal pollinators, the female flowers are not large or flamboyant, merely miniature versions of the cone that develops from the pollinated flower. Among the most attractive female flowers are the pink 'roses' produced by European larch, *Larix decidua*, which appear just before the new needles begin to sprout. Each male larch flower is small, but many are

BELOW: *This study demonstrates the great diversity of leaf shapes found among temperate plants. At the top is a leafy fringe of the huge date palm,* Phoenix dactylifera; *beneath are stately cannas; below and to the left the delicate leaves of the willow,* Salix chilensis; *on the bottom left, the geometric leaves of* Oreopanax sanderianus.

Leaf shapes
Temperate House
1 October 1991

LEFT and ABOVE: *Originating from the south-eastern and mid-western United States, tulip trees make attractive specimens in parks or large gardens. Before the leaves open out, the branching pattern can be seen quite clearly. In mid-summer, greenish cup-shaped flowers, marked with orange, open out among the leaves.*

Tulip tree, Liriodendron tulipifera, *with detail of flower*
Broad Walk
10 May 1991 (tree), 3 July 1991 (flower)

grouped into a catkin or, in the case of larch, a flattened disc. When the wind blows, or a branch is knocked, a yellow pollen cloud is produced. This can be seen quite clearly among pines.

Many trees produce copious lightweight microscopic pollen grains because it is a chancy affair whether some will land on the female flowers. Deciduous shrubs and trees, such as hazel, *Corylus avellana*, and oaks produce their catkins before or just as the leaves open, so that the pollen can be carried more easily through the branches. Goat willow, *Salix capraea*, also flowers in early spring in the Cottage Grounds, producing much larger, sticky pollen grains that are dispersed by insect visitors. Early butterflies on the wing, such as commas and small tortoiseshells, can often be seen feeding on goat willow flowers.

Magnolias, both deciduous and evergreen, have been planted in many parts of the Gardens; the mound on which the Temple of Aeolus is sited is

ABOVE: *Purple toothwort is one of several parasitic flowering plants which can be found at Kew. Now naturalized in parts of Britain, it is native to certain areas of southern Europe where it grows on poplar and willow roots. Deep purple flowers appear just above the soil in spring and, if tapped when fully open, a cream-coloured pollen cloud is produced.*

Purple toothwort, Lathraea clandestina, *on black walnut roots*
Woodland Garden
18 April 1991

enlivened by these trees blooming in spring. They produce solitary, often fragrant, flowers and the showiest of them all are the large-flowered decid-uous ones which bloom before the leaves open. After the white starry flowers of *Magnolia stellata* from Japan have faded, the outsized pink blooms of *M. campbellii* and *M. veitchii* open in a grouped planting to the west of Princess Walk. If a frost occurs after magnolia flowers have opened, their splendour is suddenly lost as the petals turn brown. On the other hand, the cream, fragrant flowers produced by the evergreen, *M. grandiflora*, do not open until well into summer. This glossy-leaved magnolia comes from the south-east of the United States, where it can grow into a pyramidal tree up to 25 metres (82 feet) high. In Britain, it is most often trained against a south-facing wall as is the case on the front of Cambridge Cottage and on either side of the entrance to the Herbarium.

The tulip tree, also a member of the magnolia family, produces cup-shaped green-yellow flowers marked with orange in mid-summer well after the leaves have developed. This large hardwood tree grows in forests in eastern North America alongside hickory, sweetgum, maple, oak and elm.

Most insect-pollinated tree flowers are colourful and showy, producing nectar to attract their pollinators. Flowers of trees from the rose family, including hawthorns (*Crataegus*), apples (*Malus*), and pears (*Pyrus*) all attract bees. At Kew, these trees are grouped together in an area between the Temperate House and the Pagoda. Bees do not fly in the rain, so if wet weather persists for several days when these flowers are out, only a small proportion will be pollinated.

The path from Cumberland Gate leads past the Herbaceous Ground and Rock Garden on the right, and the Temple of Aeolus and the Woodland Garden on the left. Leafy canopies of deciduous oaks and birches in the Woodland Garden cast shadows on the ground, creating ideal conditions for shade-loving plants such as anemones, primulas, hellebores and North American trilliums. Beneath a large black walnut tree two kinds of toothwort flowers appear without any leaves in April. Since these plants contain no green colouring (chlorophyll), they cannot manufacture their own food, so they live as parasites on tree roots. Purple toothwort, *Lathraea clandestina*, a native of southern Europe, has deep purple flowers, while *L. squamaria* bears a tall, pinkish flower spike. Both species attract bumblebees.

Pines and other conifers can be seen at Kew in an area west of the Temperate House and south of the Lake. Among the spruces is Norway spruce, *Abies picea*, the tree most likely to be brought as a Christmas tree in Britain, although one in four trees sold by the Forestry Commission are now Scots pines, *Pinus sylvestris*. The latter have softer needles and are less prone to needle drop once the tree has been felled. In Scotland Douglas firs, *Pseudotsuga menziesii*, are often sold as Christmas trees. Prince Albert initiated the tradition of decorating a tree for Christmas when he had one dispatched from Germany in 1841, much to the delight of Queen Victoria and their children.

To the right of the path beside the Waterlily Pond are a group of evergreen shrubs resembling yews with outsized needles which bear brown olive-shaped fruits in autumn. These are Chinese plum yews, *Cephalotaxus fortunei*,

LEFT: *The Chinese plum yew is a small tree with longer and glossier leaves than the European yew. In its native northern China, it can reach up to 20 metres (60 feet) high, whereas the largest recorded specimen in Britain is a mere 9 metres (27 feet) high.*

Chinese plum yew, Cephaloxtaxus
  fortunei
Arboretum
6 November 1991

ABOVE: *At first green, cedar cones gradually enlarge and turn brown to resemble a row of owls sitting on a branch. The delicate frosty coating seen on these cones quickly melted when warmed by the sun's rays. This cedar originates from the Atlas Mountains in North Africa.*

Cones of the Atlas cedar, Cedrus atlantica
Arboretum
12 December 1991

named after Robert Fortune who introduced them to Britain from China in 1849. Nearby is the yew collection. European yew trees, *Taxus baccata*, long associated with churches, have a dark green foliage – almost black in certain lights. This can provide a contrasting foil when clipped as a hedge behind a colourful herbaceous border, but elsewhere in a garden can appear very sombre. The golden variegated needles of *T. baccata* 'Barronii', on the other hand, provide year-round interest. Yew seeds are contained inside brightly coloured fleshy arils; typically red, they attract birds which aid dispersal of the seeds. In the Kew collection there is also an unusual variety of the European yew, *T. baccata* 'Luteo', originating from Ireland, which produces golden yellow arils, equally attractive to birds.

For the architectural habit of large cedars to be appreciated to the full, they need to be given plenty of room as open-grown specimen trees, so that they can be viewed from any angle in any light. Over the years, gales and snow weighing heavily on branches have damaged some limbs of the Kew cedars, but several large trees can be seen on either side of the Broad Walk, as well as west and north of the Palm House.

Various kinds of hollies form an avenue along Holly Walk, running parallel with and west of the long axis of the Temperate House. Before the Kew and Richmond estates were combined, this Walk, known then as Love Lane, divided the two. The broad-based evergreen hollies now make it a fairly sombre walk, but none the less one where the variation of the leaf colour (green, golden or variegated) and leaf shape (prickly along the edges, prickly all over or smooth-edged) can be appreciated. At Christmas time holly is associated with ivy, which in recent years has become available in a large number of different varieties, all infinitely more decorative than the type which festoons the trunks of hedgerow trees. Hardy ones are grown up the eastern wall of the Herbaceous Ground, while the more tender ivies can be seen in the floral display area in the Princess of Wales Conservatory.

Many camellias and rhododendrons are grown outside, although camellia blooms, like those of the spring-flowering magnolias, are damaged by frost. Half-hardy camellias and rhododendrons are housed together with many other woody temperate plants in the Temperate House, which was completely restored during 1977–80. Over the years the light transmission had fallen as low as 28 per cent of available light on occasions but, by replacing the glazing bars with much narrower ones made of aluminium alloy, the light transmission was greatly increased. The largest plants – including a huge Chilean palm, *Jubaea chilensis*, grown from seed collected in the Andes in 1846 – remained on site during the reconstruction, swathed in polythene wraps and warmed by gas heaters. The removal of all the other plants made it possible for some beds to be increased in size and for water features to be included in the landscaping. After restoration the plants grew much better; indeed, the South African King protea, *Protea cynaroides*, responded to the improved conditions by producing its splendid, radially symmetrical flowers, a sight not seen at Kew since Victorian times.

The main axis of the Temperate House runs from north to south, with the plants now grouped in geographical regions. The moist, cooler North Wing, housing chiefly Asian plants from Malaysia, the Himalayas, China and Japan, includes a collection of tender rhododendrons from the mountainous regions of New Guinea. The warmer (and drier) South Wing simulates a Mediterranean climate and houses plants from this region, as well as from Africa. Within the Main Block are plants native to Mauritius, Hawaii, Australia and temperate parts of Central and South America. There are several large trees here, including non-hardy palms. One quarter of the Main Block contains Australian trees, including a banyan tree, *Ficus macrophylla*, from New South Wales and Queensland and a group of tree ferns. The crowns of these ferns can be viewed from above by climbing the spiral staircase to the gallery which runs around the Main Block.

Many species of fuchsia are planted on either side of the central path, including *Fuchsia coccinea* from Chile. When this plant was crossed with other South American fuchsias, spectacular garden hybrids resulted. Also in the Main Block a crepe myrtle, *Lagerstroemia indica*, puts on a showy display of deep pink flowers for a few brief weeks.

Each wing is connected to the Main Block by a small octagon: the north one houses plants from New Zealand, Tasmania and Lord Howe Island, while the south one contains representative plants from South Africa, notably proteas and heaths from the Cape. The range of plants from so many different countries ensures that there is always something of interest to see in the Temperate House. The steps outside to the west lead down to the Australian

ABOVE: *Even though the cinnamon-coloured bark is not unattractive, the bare winter skeletons of crepe myrtle trees are transformed after the dark green leaves and deep pink crinkled petals unfurl in late summer. A native of China, crepe myrtle thrives in sub-tropical climates and, since it flowers on the new season's growth, it is often pruned hard back each year. When planted as an avenue, it may be pollarded.*

Crepe myrtle, Lagerstroemia indica
Temperate House

BELOW: *A range of South African ericas and proteas is grown in the South Octagon of the Temperate House. This heath exists in a great variety of colours, including pale yellow as shown here, pink, brown and white.*

A Cape heath, Erica longifolia
Temperate House
9 August 1991

ABOVE: *The magnificent radially symmetrical flowers – up to 20 cm (8 inches) in diameter – of the king protea are produced on a comparatively small bush, 1–2 metres (3–6 feet) high.*

King or giant protea, Protea cynaroides
Temperate House
23 May 1991

House, the first aluminium house to be erected at Kew. It should not be missed in winter, when the wattles (*Acacia* spp.), boronias, cassias and coreas are flowering.

Visitors to Kew are inevitably attracted to brightly coloured exotica, but many temperate forest plants are well worth a closer look. Britain's island climate and the ameliorating effect of the North Atlantic Drift (Gulf Stream), enable a large proportion of temperate plants from northern and southern hemispheres to be grown outside in gardens or in cool greenhouses.

CHAPTER THREE

TROPICAL FOREST PLANTS

*It is estimated that tropical
rainforests contain at least half of all species
living on earth today. The Palm
House provides a unique opportunity to see
the largest display of threatened
rainforest plants anywhere in Europe, and
Kew's scientists are making a
tremendous contribution to their conservation.*

BATHED IN A warm, humid atmosphere all year round, tropical rain-forests are the most diverse of any ecosystem on earth. It is now recognized that these areas do not just represent a unique and rich collection of plants and animals, they are also essential in helping to maintain the natural climatic balance of life on earth. In addition they contain a vast reservoir of virtually untapped natural resources.

By no means all tropical forests are wet; dry forests also exist. Together they lie within a very patchy equatorial band between the Tropics of Cancer and Capricorn. Trees in the dry forests may shed their leaves during the dry season and they do not reach such huge dimensions as the rainforest giants. The canopy is open and the diversity of species within these forests is not so great as within rainforests. Some two thirds of tropical dry forest occurs in Africa, with several areas in Latin America and the rest in Asia and on Pacific islands.

Trees of tropical moist forests, on the other hand, are evergreen and they form a closed canopy, for their crowns spread out so that they almost touch

LEFT: *Shafts of sunlight stream on to the rich evergreen
tropical rainforest at Monteverde Forest Reserve in Costa
Rica in April. Tree trunks, clothed with epiphytic
mosses, provide support for robust climbers, while tree
ferns form part of the understorey.*

one another. When a giant tree falls, it creates a gap in the canopy through which a shaft of sunlight beams onto the forest floor. The light stimulates rapid growth of tree seedlings, only one of which will untimately reach maturity to fill the gap. Photographs of the overhead canopy taken with a 180° fish-eye lens produce circular pictures, which can be used to determine the proportion of light reaching the rainforest floor. It was found that some 30 per cent of sky can be seen where a big gap is created by a recently fallen tree but, by the time the canopy is closed, this is reduced to a mere 6 per cent.

During the last decade a great deal of information about life in the rain-forest canopy has been gained by pioneering work using lightweight mountaineering equipment to make aerial walkways. From these biologists have been able to study, at first hand, the role arboreal animals play within the canopy community, including the dispersal of fruits produced high above the forest floor.

This chapter concentrates on rainforest flora, since Kew has such a large and important collection of these plants – many now endangered. It is a sobering thought that, although tropical rainforests cover only some 7 per cent of the land surface, it is estimated that they contain at least half of all species living on earth today. These forests occur in Central and South America, Africa, Indo-Malaysia, Papua New Guinea and Australia.

However, devastating destruction by the hand of man during the latter part of this century has kept these habitats constantly in the news. The statistics make for grim reading. Using mainly remote sensing techniques from satellites, backed up by some ground surveying, the Food and Agricultural Organization (FAO) estimates that some 11 million hectares (over 27 million acres) of tropical forests, including rainforests, dry forests and bamboos, were lost in 1980, and their 1990 survey calculates a 35 per cent increase loss to 17 million hectares (42 million acres). In addition to destruction through clear felling and burning, forests become degraded as large timber trees are hauled out. The Worldwide Fund for Nature (WWF) estimates that up to 20 million hectares (almost 50 million acres) of tropical forests, an area more than twice the size of Austria, may be lost or degraded each year. If the present rate of destruction continues unabated, all rainforests will have been destroyed forever by the middle of the next century.

Over the years Kew has played a key role in disseminating knowledge about these priceless habitats. As collectors brought back many plants new to science, they were propagated and distributed around the world. One of the most famous translocations was the introduction of the rubber tree, *Hevea brasiliensis*, to Asia via Kew. Long before Europeans discovered rubber, American Indians made balls and crude shoes from the milky latex produced by this member of the spurge family, Euphorbiaceae. All rubber came from wild trees growing in South America until Henry Wickham collected 70,000 seeds from Brazil and brought them to Kew in 1876. The germination rate was low: only 2,397 plants were raised in glasshouses cleared of orchids to make room for the tropical seedlings. Most of these were shipped to Ceylon (now Sri Lanka), in thirty-eight Wardian cases (miniature portable glass cases which could be placed out on a ship's deck). Somewhat later, the extensive rubber plantations of Malaysia – now the world's leading supplier of rubber – were developed from just twenty-two seedlings. More recently, life-saving drugs have been discovered from rainforest plants (see p.146) by scientists working in the Jodrell Laboratory at Kew. Tropical rainforests may seem very far removed from Kew Gardens, but facets of them have been recreated

RIGHT: *For rainforest plants to survive, Kew has had to re-create the hot, humid atmosphere of their native habitat. Here a tree fern from Papua New Guinea looms out of the mist in the Wet Tropics section of the Princess of Wales Conservatory.*

Tree fern, Cyathea fugax
Princess of Wales Conservatory, Wet Tropics section
26 June 1989

in the Palm House and the wet tropical section of the Princess of Wales Conservatory. These are by far the two most congenial places to be at Kew on a cold, wet day; whereas on a hot day, most visitors find the extremely hot and humid conditions more than they can bear even for a brief spell. Yet only by providing these conditions can plants of the moist tropical regions thrive, flower and ultimately set fruit.

With the exception of the Nash Conservatory (formerly the Aroid House), the Palm House is the oldest glasshouse at Kew. The most famous curvilinear glasshouse in the world, as well as the largest, it has often been credited solely to the architect Decimus Burton because only his initials were on the plans. In fact, it was Richard Turner, an ironmaster and engineer from Dublin, who put forward the innovative idea of using a wrought-iron framework for the main arches in preference to the much heavier cast-iron frame. Wrought iron had been used in shipbuilding, but this was the first time it had been proposed for the large spans to support a glasshouse. The increased strength did away

LEFT: *These fan palms are grown in the north wing of the Palm House, so that when the sun is out during the afternoon it shines down through the leaves.* Pritchardia arecina *is found only on the island of Maui in the Hawaiian group.*

Fan palms, Pritchardia lanaiensis *and*
  P. arecina
Palm House
13 March 1991

RIGHT: *This palm is native to Java and Sumatra where it grows beneath the huge rainforest trees as part of the understorey. At Kew, it is grown in the Wet Tropics section of the Conservatory. The fruits are borne on a colourful branch well below the overhanging leaves.*

Palm bearing fruit, Pinanga coronata
Princess of Wales Conservatory, Wet Tropics
  section
3 September 1991

with the need for a forest of internal pillars, as drawn in Burton's initial plans, so resulting in a spacious area for displaying plants; while Burton's decision to site the Palm House next to the Pond meant that the exterior could be appreciated as a double image when seen reflected in the water.

The Palm House was built during the period 1844–8, primarily to house the palms coming into Europe during the early part of Queen Victoria's reign. In 1768 only six species of palms were grown at Kew, by 1830 there were 40 species, and by 1882 the collection had increased more than tenfold to 420 species. At first, with the exception of a bed for growing climbers around each pillar supporting the raised walkway, the plants were grown in teak tubs or pots set on iron gratings or on raised benches in the apse ends. However, when it was found that many did not flourish, beds were constructed during the winter of 1859–60 in the central transept. Nowadays, nearly all the plants – apart from some in the apse ends of the north and south wings – are grown in the beds.

Since it was built the Palm House has been restored twice, first between 1955 and 1957 and again between 1984 and 1988. Structural alterations made during the 1950s restoration affected the air circulation in such a way that condensation on the glass resulted in corrosion of the glazing bars. So the Palm House became unsafe and had to be closed to the public in 1984. Before the last restoration began, 1,000 plants had to be removed; some were housed elsewhere while others were propagated. Improvements made during the 1980s restoration included deep beds in both the north and south wings, as well as soil-warming devices and an automatic humidifying system. Even so, hand spraying is still carried out several times a day in summer to prevent the plants drying out. As you enter through any of the Palm House's four doors, you leave behind a conventional English garden scene with roses on one side and formal bedding on the other, both offset by lawns, and plunge into the steamy, tropical atmosphere where the temperature never drops below 15°C (59°F), nor the humidity below 75 per cent.

ABOVE: *Prior to the 1980s restoration of the Palm House, the jade vine flowered well, but it was to be another ten years (in 1991) before its exquisite flowers were seen again at Kew. Confined to the Philippines, the rough woody stem twines and twists like a rope as it climbs up tall trees towards the light in damp forests. In the tropics, the jade vine is cultivated over trellises in a similar way to laburnum in temperate gardens.*

Jade vine, Strongylodon macrobotrys
Palm House
12 April 1991

LEFT: *Passion flowers are tropical and sub-tropical climbers that produce showy and elaborate flowers.* Passiflora quadrangularis *from tropical South America is no exception. The showy purplish flowers hang down from the vine, edged with white- and purple-banded filaments not unlike the tentacles of a sea anemone. This passion flower is unusual in having four-angled stems with obvious wings. Both the fleshy root and the yellow-green fruits, 12–25 centimetres (5–10 inches) in length, are edible.*

Giant granadilla, Passiflora quadrangularis
Princess of Wales Conservatory, Ornamental section
26 June 1989

Over the years, the range of plants on display has changed. Today, we no longer see many bougainvilleas and other colourful exotic cultivars; instead the collection contains an important gene pool of endangered rainforest plants as well as plants of economic value. They include palms, cycads, screw-pines, vines, bananas and giant bamboos, all competing with one another for space and light. The flowers of some climbers, notably aristolochias and passion-flowers, are often high up on the vines where there is more direct light than among the lush growth at ground level.

The natural sounds of the rainforest fauna are sadly missing, although the lack of pungent odours from over-ripe fruit is, perhaps, a bonus. For example, when the ripe fruit of the durian, *Durio zibethinus*, splits, it releases a potent smell resembling a mixture of rancid butter, bad drains and stale beer! Yet the fleshy aril around each seed is reputedly quite delectable and sweet-tasting. However, the vibrant colours of many rainforest flowers are certainly there – hibiscus, heliconias, *Costus*, passionflowers and jade vine, to name but a few.

ABOVE: *Cotton is one of many plants of economic value grown in the Palm House. Comparison of its flower shape with that of the larger and more colourful Hibiscus flowers nearby confirms that they both belong to the same family – the Malvaceae. After pollination, a capsule is produced, inside which masses of fine white hairs develop on the surface of the seeds.*

Cotton flower, Gossypicum *sp.*
Palm House
10 October 1991

RIGHT: *The calico flower is such a vigorous climber that you almost need a pair of binoculars to appreciate the curious flowers produced high up the vine among kidney-shaped leaves. Opening out from an inflated tube is a cup-shaped hollow, coloured maroon with white marbling, in which the nectar is found. Flies, attracted to the flower by its smell, crawl into the cup. Once inside, a mass of downward-pointing hairs prevent the flies from crawling back out; when the flower withers, they escape and cross-pollinate the next flower they visit.*

Calico flower, Aristolochia elegans
Palm House
14 October 1991

49

During Victorian times the Palm House proved to be a great draw simply by housing collections of bizarre palms, cycads, and a limited range of other tropical plants. Palms and cycads may look similar, each bearing frond-like leaves, but they are not even distantly related. Cycads are often referred to as living fossils, for they represent the remnants of an ancient flora which flourished during the age of the dinosaurs in the Triassic period, some 200 million years ago. They are the most primitive of all living seed-producing plants and those which still survive all come from the tropics and sub-tropics. Like conifers, cycads produce cones which bear naked seeds, unenclosed within ovaries; and, like yew and holly, cycads have separate male and female plants.

Even though palms are an ancient group of plants, with fossil records dating back to the Upper Cretaceous period, they have much more highly evolved flowers and fruits than cycads and are classed together with grasses and lilies as monocotyledons. Most palms have either fan-shaped or finely divided pinnate leaves.

ABOVE: *Brought back to England in 1775 by Francis Masson, one of Kew's earliest collectors, this cycad is reputedly the oldest pot plant in the world. Now in its third century, it has developed a prostrate habit, so it has to be supported from beneath.*

Cycad, Encephalartos altensteinii
Palm House
4 October 1991

ABOVE RIGHT: *Extending from Queensland and New Guinea to various Pacific islands, the Cape York lily is found along rainforest margins, often among rocks. The flower spike, which grows up to 30 centimetres (1 foot), has conspicuous bracts, green below and rose above. It belongs to the ginger family and the dried rhizomes of a related species,* Curcuma longa *(formerly called C.* domestica*), yield turmeric which is used as a spice, as a yellow cloth dye and as a food colourant.*

Cape York lily, Curcuma australasica
Palm House
9 August 1991

From both an economic and an aesthetic point of view, palms are extremely important. In their native lands the leaves are used for shelter, clothing, brushes, baskets and fans, while palm trunks provide fuel and building piles. Other products originating from palms and used worldwide include dates, raffia and rattan. Coconut palms, *Cocos nucifera*, provide coir from the husk around the fruit used to make matting and ropes, as well as a substitute for natural peat (see p.20), while the dried flesh of the fruit itself provides copra. Oil from both the coconut palm and the African oil palm, *Elaeis guineensis*, is used in the manufacture of soaps. Larger palms can make majestic avenues, as for example the royal palms, *Roystonea regia*, planted in the botanic gardens of Mauritius in the Indian Ocean.

The first plant to be brought back into the restored Palm House when it was replanted in 1989 was considerably older than the building itself. *Encephalartos altensteinii* (formerly *E. longifolius*), a cycad which has been pot-bound since 1775, is almost certainly the oldest pot plant anywhere in the world. It was collected from the eastern cape of South Africa in the 1770s and brought to England by Francis Masson, one of Kew's earliest collectors. The bicentenary of this aged cycad was commemorated in 1975 when Kew exhibited a photograph of it on their stand at the Royal Horticultural Society's Annual Show at Chelsea. Estimated now to weigh some 3 tonnes, the cycad's horizontal trunk has to be supported from beneath. Measuring 4 metres (13 feet) from the base to the growing point, the plant has grown, on average, 2.5 centimetres (1 inch) per year.

When the glasshouse was replanted in 1989 following its restoration, it was arranged as ecological displays from distinct geographic areas. The south wing houses African rainforest plants, and the north wing plants from Asia, Australasia and the Pacific. The beds in the central transept contain rainforest plants from the Americas, with the tallest palms planted here. As might be expected, palms are especially well represented and some are illustrated on pp. 46 and 47. Even though the Palm House is not tall enough to house the giant trees of the rainforest, it does contain the largest ecological display of threatened rainforest plants anywhere in Europe.

BELOW: *Even though the Guinea chestnut flowers at Kew over a period of several months, each flower fades very soon after opening. The creamy petals form an erect pod-like bud and, as they unfurl, hundreds of stamens emerge, cream at the base and rose above, each topped with an orange anther. Within a day, the whole flower turns foxy-brown and droops.*

Guinea chestnut, Pachira aquatica
Princess of Wales Conservatory, Wet Tropics section
9 September 1991

BELOW: *This endangered palm is the sole species of a genus endemic to the Seychelles, where it is known as* latanier latte. *Conspicuous prop roots develop at the bottom of the stem which help to support it. Above are rings of large downward-pointing black spines which appear at the top of the trunk on older palms. Split sections of the trunk are used as rain gutters.*

Prop roots of latanier latte palm, Verschaffeltia splendida
Palm House
14 October 1991

The best way of appreciating how rainforest vegetation is stratified into distinct layers, with the herbs and young seedlings on the ground and the climbers and the trees above, is by ascending the spiral staircase to walk around the upper gallery of the centre transept. Indeed, this is the only way to see palm crowns and the giant bamboo leaves (see p.122). Before the Palm House could be restored, the mature palms had to be felled and it will be a couple of decades before the new ones attain the same height.

Even though the bananas, *Musa* spp. and their relatives, the heliconias, originate from opposite sides of the globe, they frequent similar niches in the wild, so it is appropriate they should share the same bed in the central transept. Here they produce a succession of colourful and dramatic flowers throughout the British summer.

Surprisingly these outsized – some even gigantic – perennial herbs have a stem made simply from the ensheathing leaf bases. A relative, the traveller's palm *Ravelana madagascarensis*, growing in the south end of the Palm House opposite the potted cycads, has a true stem. Bananas frequent more open parts of their native forest such as clearings, forest margins and any disturbed areas. They originate from Indo-Malaysia where the true species are pollinated by insects and bats, but the bananas (eaten raw) and the plantains (usually eaten cooked) so widely consumed today have been produced as a result of hybridization and cannot produce seeds. Unripe fruits are rich in starch and bitter to taste but, as they ripen, the starch is converted to sugar and they become sweeter. It is probable that Arab traders, who regularly plied back and forth across the Indian Ocean in their dhows, brought the banana to Africa via Madagascar (Malagasy Republic), perhaps as early as 400 AD. It is known that the Portuguese introduced it to the Canary Islands around 1510, from where it was taken to South America. We cannot be sure when bananas reached Britain, but they were widely cultivated during the latter part of the nineteenth century in the heated stovehouses of the aristocracy.

Over the years Kew has been instrumental in bananas becoming the most widely produced tropical fruit. During Victorian times bananas were shipped worldwide from Kew in Wardian cases. Then, between the two World Wars, Kew was a quarantine station for several tropical crops of economic importance – including bananas – *en route* from one continent to another.

The fresh green of their new leaves brings a tropical atmosphere to any garden, although when buffeted by wind, they become shredded into narrow strips. Bananas can be grown in non-tropical gardens that experience long, hot summers, provided that the plants are protected during winter. Indeed, I have seen mummified plants in some of the classical gardens in Suzhou, China, completely swathed with sackcloth in February.

Other species grown at Kew include the velvet banana *Musa velutina* (see p.54) in the north wing of the Palm House and *M. basjoo* from Japan (see p.142) in the Temperate House.

Heliconias, which originate from the other side of the world in the Americas, produce particularly striking and long-lasting flowers with abundant nectar which attracts their bird pollinators. The more delicate orange and yellow parrot flower can be seen in several beds in the Palm House, while the showy flowers of lobster claw, *H. rostrata*, and parrot's beak, *H. psittacorum*, are adjacent to the bananas.

Rainforests develop on a surprisingly small depth of soil, so that none of the trees produces deep roots. Additional support is provided either by means of prop roots (common among palms and screw-pines) which are particularly

LEFT: *In addition to the many kinds of edible bananas, there are also ornamental species. Indeed, the striking yellow and red flowers of the velvet banana, from Assam, were the prime reason for it being brought into cultivation in 1895. The flowers produce attractive, albeit inedible, fruit covered with pink-red velvety fur.*

Velvet banana, Musa velutina
Palm House
10 May 1991

RIGHT: *Over a period of many weeks, the star-shaped fruit of* Sterculia mexicana *gradually turns deep scarlet. When fully ripe, it splits along the inner edge to reveal large blue seeds—eagerly sought after by birds in its native Mexico. At Kew, this plant fruits in both the Palm House and the Princess of Wales Conservatory.*

Sterculia mexicana fruit
Palm House
12 June 1991

well developed on the Seychelles palm, *Verschaffeltia splendida*, planted in the Palm House central transept; or by huge fin-like buttresses (found on large hardwood trees).

A closer look at areas of bare soil in the beds may reveal the fruiting bodies of tropical fungi that appear spontaneously from time to time, the most conspicuous ones being the yellow cottony agaric, *Leucocoprinus luteus*, an inedible pan-tropical species.

Several rainforest trees develop their flowers (and fruits) directly on woody trunks or branches, a process known as cauliflory. When, in 1752, the Swedish botanist Osbeck came across a tree with flowers emerging from the trunk in East Java, he was convinced he had found a leafless parasite growing on the tree! The ancient type of heavy fruits produced by the durian and by the

ABOVE: *Dumb cane is one of several plants from tropical America, belonging to the arum family. The plant was used to punish slaves in the West Indies, who were made to bite on it. This caused the mouth to swell up, thereby rendering the person speechless for several days — hence the plant's common name.*

Dumb cane, Dieffenbachia sequinae reginae
Princess of Wales Conservatory, Tropical Ferns section
24 September 1991

ABOVE LEFT: Goethea strictifolia *is a shrub from Brazil that bears its numerous flowers directly on the trunks – a feature known as cauliflory. It is the crimson bracts (arranged in the shape of a bell), rather than the smaller white flowers within them, that attract the eye.*

Goethea strictifolia
Palm House
12 June 1991

ABOVE RIGHT: *African violets, which are one of the most popular of all houseplants, originate from a single mountain range in Tanzania. This plant is one of several true species from which the many hybrids have been bred to produce a whole range of colours from pale purple, dark purple, pink to white, as well as double and bi-coloured flowers. These plants are easily propagated by means of leaf cuttings.*

African violet, Saintpaulia intermedia
Princess of Wales Conservatory, Wet Tropics section
10 May 1991

cannonball tree, *Couroupita guianensis*, cannot be supported on slender twigs, hence their development on the trunks themselves. Cauliflorous plants which flower in the Palm House include cocoa, *Theobroma cacao*, which flowers in late summer, and *Goethea strictiflora*.

The varied ways in which rainforest plants are pollinated and their fruits dispersed are gradually being pieced together, but with such a rich flora – often not readily accessible – there is much still to unravel. Insects, birds and mammals all play their part in aiding cross-pollination from one flower to another. Bird flowers open by day, are brightly coloured (many are red, including *Hibiscus* spp., *Erythrina* spp. and silk cotton, *Bombax ceiba*) and produce copious watery nectar. Bat flowers, on the other hand, open at dusk, produce viscid nectar and a musky scent; they are large and strong as they have to support the weight of a bat as it feeds. The spectacular flowers of the cannonball tree are bat pollinated, as are those of the Asian durian trees.

Agile arboreal climbers, such as monkeys, play an important role in the dispersal of rainforest plants. Once fruits ripen on a tree, monkeys soon home in and gorge themselves. Bats and birds such as toucans (in South America) and hornbills (in Old World tropics) which fly from one food source to another, can disperse seed over a much wider area than monkeys. Fruits accidentally dropped by monkeys and bats, or which fall naturally to the forest floor, are eagerly eaten by ground-dwelling mammals such as tapirs and peccaries in South America.

The Amazon basin is a floodplain which is covered by water for up to seven months of the year. The ripening of the fruits of many trees and vines is synchronized with the floods, so that they are dispersed by water, by monkeys or by fish. Howler, squirrel and uakari monkeys all feed on fruit, the bald-headed uakaris moving from tree to tree just above the flood water. But none of these terrestrial mammals is such an effective dispersal agent of large, hard fruits as the tambaqui, a 1-metre- (3-feet) long fish that invades the flooded forest. Huge molars in their large jaws enable these fish to crack the hard nuts of the rubber trees. When the fruit is ripe, the fish swim around beneath the trees waiting for the distinctive plop as each one falls into the water.

Many ornamental tropical bromeliads flower in the hot and humid conditions provided under glass at Kew. In the wild, these plants grow as epiphytes, perching high up on branches of South American rainforest trees where they gain more light than at ground level.

ABOVE: Aechmea nidularoides
23 May 1991

LEFT: Neoregelia concentrica
7 July 1989

Princess of Wales Conservatory

Some rainforest trees and climbers are dispersed by means of winged fruits and seeds which spiral or float down from high above the floor. Many familiar herbaceous plants of temperate gardens have sepals (the outer parts of the flower that protect the bud) which either drop off as the flower opens (such as in poppies) or wither (such as in sweet peas) but on certain tropical forest trees they grow after pollination to produce pronounced wings on the fruits. Among these are some of the dipterocarp trees from Asia, like *Shorea*, three of whose original five sepals on each flower grow into wings. As the fruit falls from a large tree it initially drops vertically for some 2 metres (6½ feet), before it begins to spin and slow down. This increases the fruit's chance of being blown away from the parent tree before it hits the ground. If any of these winged fruits should happen to land on moving water, the fruit floats with the wings erect and is carried downstream. However, if the wind happens to be blowing upstream, the winged sepals act as sails carrying the fruits upstream against the current.

Some plants, such as the climbing shrub, *Alsomitra*, produce seeds surrounded by large wafer-thin extensions that also function to slow down the rate of descent which follows a zig-zagging path.

As well as in the Palm House, tropical forest plants can also be seen at Kew in the Princess of Wales Conservatory where the more open interior allows for the display of tropical herbaceous plants including gingers, anthuriums, spider lilies and peppers, together with climbers such as hoyas, passionflowers and aristolochias and a few scattered tree ferns and small understorey palms. In this chapter we are concerned with the extensive Wet Tropics section, creatively landscaped on different levels with several areas of open water, one of which contains a hybrid of the giant Amazonian waterlily (see p.68), and the smaller Tropical Ferns section which houses many ferns, as well as orchids and other epiphytic plants.

Among the rainforest plants on display in the Wet Tropics section, are some familiar as house plants: African violets (*Saintpaulia* spp.), marantas with their attractively patterned leaves and bromeliads from Central and South America. In addition there are several plants of economic value, including fruits (bananas and pineapple) as well as spices (pepper and ginger).

Bromeliads have a rosette of leaves, from the centre of which the flowers develop. Some plants grow directly on the ground, but many live by perching as epiphytes high up on rainforest trees and require a high humidity. The water contained in these rosettes provide miniature aerial aquaria in which insects – particularly mosquitos – a few frogs and even a freshwater crab can breed. The extensive bromeliad display in the Princess of Wales Conservatory, both in beds and also on simulated tree trunks, includes the urn plant *Aechmea fasciata*, neoregelias, guzmanias, billbergias, tillandsias and the earth stars *Cryptanthus* spp. with their strikingly patterned leaves. The individual flowers of most bromeliads are not particularly showy, but the plants become especially striking when the bracts radiating out from the central flowers change colour from green to red or mauve.

The first bromeliad to come to Britain was, in fact, the pineapple. This was in 1690, and by the eighteenth century ideal conditions for its growth were recreated in the heated stovehouses of many a large estate. In November and December, *Ananas comosus* var. *variegatus*, a striking ornamental relative of the pineapple, can be seen flowering in the Princess of Wales Conservatory.

Near by, clumps of the grey fine-leaved so-called Spanish moss, *Tillandsia*, hang down from artificial trees. This is not a true moss, but a flowering plant – yet another epiphytic bromeliad. Often referred to as airplants in North America, clumps of this plant festoon trees such as evergreen oaks and swamp cypresses in southern Florida and Louisiana. The dried plants were once used as vegetable hair for stuffing early car seats.

There is also an extensive collection of begonias in the Wet Tropics section: representatives from a large and important group of ornamental plants, with some 1,000 species, as well as thousands of hybrids and varieties developed by the horticultural trade. They thrive in the tropics and sub-tropics – notably in Latin America and south-east Asia – and exhibit great diversity of habit, foliage and flowers. Most are small herbaceous perennials, growing up from rhizomes or tubers, but some, such as *Begonia luxurians*, are woody and reach heights of over 4 metres (12 feet), while others are annuals. Begonia leaves are asymmetrical – one side is bigger than the other. Many are simple in form, but *B. duartei* has a spiral leaf while others are divided like a palm leaf. The flowers are either male or female, but both kinds appear on the same plant. *Begonia nitida* (*B. minor*), introduced from Jamaica in 1777, was the first begonia to be cultivated in England. It was almost a century later that *B. rex* was introduced from Assam and later hybridized to produce the range of very attractively patterned, large-leaved foliage plants – in shades of silver, pink, copper and bronze (set off against variously coloured backgrounds) – we know today.

Tropical orchids, an especially attractive group of epiphytic plants, are displayed in an adjacent area of the Princess of Wales Conservatory together with tropical ferns. Some of the orchids are permanent fixtures, but many more from the Nursery appear as temporary displays behind glass panels.

In 1974 the Convention on International Trade in Endangered Species of Wild Fauna and Flora (CITES) was set up to control and monitor trade in endangered wild animals and plants. None the less, orchids and other plants much prized by collectors are still illegally imported to Britain. Plants that

RIGHT: *The exquisite flowers of this slipper orchid reach up to 30 centimetres (1 foot) in diameter. Over-collecting has resulted in it being confined to two sites on the lower flanks of Mount Kinabalu in Sabah, so that it is now one of the rarest plants in the world. In the wild, it grows on ledges of steep slopes close to water, where it receives bright reflected light.*

Slipper orchid, Paphiopedilum
  rothschildianum
Nursery
7 May 1991

BELOW: *Unlike commercial pineapples which have uniform green leaves, this ornamental variety has cream borders. In addition, it produces a striking scarlet inflorescence in the centre of the leaf rosette. These plants grow with their roots in the ground, not as epiphytes up trees like many other tropical bromeliads.*

Variegated pineapple, Ananas comosus *var.*
  variegatus
Princess of Wales Conservatory, Wet Tropics section
11 October 1991

This spread illustrates some of the many tropical begonias grown under glass in the Wet Tropics section of the Princess of Wales Conservatory.

LEFT: *Papua New Guinea is the home of this begonia with arching stems bearing deeply lobed and toothed bronze leaves with red spots. The habit and the deep pink flowers make this an ideal plant for hanging baskets in the tropics or in the greenhouse.*

Pink spot begonia, Begonia serratipetala. *27 June 1991*

have been confiscated by HM Customs and Excise are sometimes sent to Kew for identification and propagation. In 1985 a massive consignment (3,500 plants of eighty species) of epiphytic orchids from Mexico was intercepted at Heathrow. After holding them in quarantine, Kew distributed many of these plants to other botanical gardens. Rare species are propagated at Kew, although this is not permitted until after any pending court case has been heard, because the evidence must be left intact. Plants held under the CITES regulations cannot be distributed until they are released for normal propagation, but many other rare plants are propagated and distributed to aid in their conservation.

As we gaze and marvel at the infinite range of tropical forest plants assembled from across the globe, we should not forget those intrepid explorers who often suffered not only hardships and discomforts but also sometimes ill-health in their quest to find plants new to science. Notable early naturalist explorers include H.E. Bates, working within the Amazonian rainforest around the middle of the last century, and Alfred Russel Wallace, who travelled in South America from 1848 to 1852 and to the Malay archipelago from 1854 to 1862. Perhaps even more remarkable were the journeys made by a middle-aged Victorian lady. For fourteen years from 1871 Marianne North travelled the world, painting exquisite scenes and floral portraits at a time when photography was not widely used. Sometimes her paintings depicted a bird or butterfly pollinator on the flower. Four of the plants she painted were unknown to science and named after her. One, *Crinum northianum* from Borneo, was described from her drawings – proof of just how accurate they were. The Marianne North Gallery in Kew Gardens houses 832 of her paintings and 246 different types of wood she collected on her travels.

More recently Margaret Mee painted and collected extensively in South America. She preferred to paint orchids, heliconias and bromeliads, because they would flower after collection and so she could continue working on them in her Rio de Janeiro studio. On her tragic accidental death in November 1988, Margaret Mee left an important legacy – of considerable scientific

BELOW: *This upright begonia from Chile and Brazil can reach almost 2 metres (6 feet) in height. Each umbrella-like leaf has up to seventeen toothed leaflets which are red and hairy above and green below.*

Palm-leaf begonia, Begonia luxurians *2 August 1991*

value – of the Amazon forest flora, with more than 400 gouache portraits, some fifteen diaries and twenty-five sketchbooks she had amassed during her thirty-five years' work.

While the location and habits of most plants grown in the Palm House have been known for some time, the full economic value of many rainforest plants has become appreciated only comparatively recently (see p.146). The demise of the rainforests has provided added impetus for discovering new methods of storing their seeds so that they remain viable. Normally kept permanently damp in their natural habitat, they die when dried and so cannot be stored in the same way as other seeds in Kew's Seed Bank.

If rainforests continue to be destroyed at the alarming rate we have witnessed in recent years, the microcosm reproduced at Kew will be among the few places left where we can observe and appreciate an infinitesimal part of their former diversity.

BELOW: *The puckered Nile-green leaves bearing a dark reddish-brown cross make this begonia quite distinctive. Indeed, since it seldom flowers, it is primarily grown for its fine foliage. A native of south-east Asia, it was introduced to the West via Singapore.*

Iron cross begonia, Begonia masoniana
10 May 1991

CHAPTER FOUR

AQUATIC PLANTS

*Outdoor ponds and lakes, with
their associated flora and fauna, have been a
feature of Kew from its very earliest
days. Add to these the displays of tropical and
mangrove swamp plants as well as
the recently opened marine exhibits, and it
becomes possible for visitors to see
plants from freshwater and marine habitats
continents apart.*

THE GIANT Amazonian waterlily, papyrus and duckweed may live continents apart, but they all share one common factor – water, or to be more specific, freshwater. Many of the fastest growing plants in the world are native of wetlands, which can be eight times as productive as a wheatfield monoculture. Marginal plants help to stabilize river and stream banks, while open water aquatics provide a food source for aquatic herbivores, ranging in size from pond snails to manatees.

While the area covered by freshwater habitats is infinitesimal compared to the extent – some 70 per cent – of the earth engulfed by seawater, only the shallow, clear, unpolluted seas contain larger marine algae or seaweeds, which require light to grow. But even clear seawater absorbs light so rapidly that 1 metre (3 feet) down more than half the sunlight beaming on the surface has been lost. Since the long wavelengths (reds and oranges) are absorbed most quickly, photographs taken underwater by natural light have a bluish-green cast, eliminated only by using artificial light.

Until 1991 marine algae could not be seen at Kew, but in the summer of that year, an innovative exhibit – the first in the world specifically designed

LEFT: *This shallow pond within Hampshire's New Forest supports a variety of aquatic plants. By late summer the yellow flags,* Iris pseudacorus, *have faded, but bur-reed,* Sparganium sp., *and white waterlilies,* Nymphaea alba, *are both in bloom. The red-leafed plant around the margins is Hampshire purslane,* Ludwigia palustris.

LEFT: *Yellow flag is one of several wetland plants native to Britain and Europe grown in the Aquatic Garden. Each spring, green strap-shaped leaves grow up from the rhizomes before the yellow flowers – the fleur-de-lis of heraldry – open and are visited by bumblebees.*

Yellow flag, Iris pseudacorus
Aquatic Garden
8 June 1991

BELOW: *Nearly all the* Nuphar *water-lilies, from the temperate zone of the northern hemisphere, have yellow flowers which are held well above the water. Each flower has five to twelve thick yellow petal-like sepals inside which are smaller petals. Like the yellow waterlily,* Nuphar lutea, *from Europe, this lily from Japan has flask-shaped fruits.*

Nuphar japonicum
Aquatic Garden
7 June 1991

for this group of plants – was opened in the basement of the reconstructed Palm House. Hardy freshwater plants are grown in the open at Kew in the Aquatic Garden, in the Waterlily Pond and around the margins of the Palm House Pond and the Lake. Tropical aquatics, on the other hand, are housed in the Waterlily House and the Princess of Wales Conservatory, together with plants of mangrove swamps.

Among the aquatic plants grown at Kew are species that have been collected from their natural habitats or grown from seed, as well as some cultivars available through the horticultural trade. Thus a Japanese waterlily with yellow flowers – *Nuphar japonicum* – may come to share a pool with water soldier, *Stratiotes aloides*, from Europe and the blue-flowered pickerel weed, *Pontederia cordata*, from North America.

The Aquatic Garden was made in 1909 for hardy water and marsh plants. It is a sunken formal area with five water-filled tanks and two rectangular beds for marsh plants. The large, central, oval tank is raised above the sunken paths – a feature which the garden designer, Gertrude Jekyll, greatly approved from the standpoint of safety to children.

Many plants in the four corner tanks of the Aquatic Garden are familiar ones from British and European wetlands: for example, marsh marigold, *Caltha palustris*; yellow flag, *Iris pseudacorus*; reedmace, *Typha* spp. (often erroneously referred to as bulrush) and bogbean, *Menyanthes trifoliata*. There is also an opportunity to see the beautiful flowering rush, *Butomus umbellatus*, now very local in Britain as canal and river margins have been cleaned up and ponds infilled. Not a true rush, the plant produces an umbel of pink flowers on a tall stem well above the water.

The two damp beds contain many British marsh plants such as rushes (*Juncus* spp.), dropworts (*Oenanthe* spp.), valerians (*Valeriana* spp.) and mints (*Mentha* spp.). Within the central pool are several dozen species, varieties and cultivars of waterlilies that are hardy in Britain, their radially symmetrical flowers opening fully only on bright sunny days. Waterlilies can also be seen in the Waterlily Pond, which was made from a disused gravel pit in 1897. Coots will sometimes make a floating nest among the lily pads here.

A few unusual aquatics from high latitudes can be seen in the Alpine House. These include an arctic waterlily, *Nymphaea tetragona*, in the small pool fed by a waterfall. From high altitude in Lesotho, there is the aquatic *Aponogeton ranunculiflorus*, growing in a pot of water plunged into the refrigerated bench.

Beside the east end of the Palm House Pond is a stand of waterside plants with outsized leaves resembling umbrellas blown inside out. These gunneras, *Gunnera chilensis* and *G. tinctoria* are related to *G. manicata* from southern Brazil, where it grows in gulleys among rotting leaves. In ideal conditions it can produce leaves over 2.5 metres (8 feet) across, but even at somewhat less than 2 metres ($6\frac{1}{2}$ feet), they are still the largest leaves that can be grown in temperate zones. When frosted, gunneras die down to the ground and, because they are not hardy, the crowns need to be protected by a covering of old leaves and bracken.

There was great excitement in the Gardens when the giant Amazonian waterlily (then known as *Victoria regia* in honour of Queen Victoria) first flowered in June 1850, although Kew was not the first place in Britain to flower this spectacular aquatic plant. That honour went to Sir Joseph Paxton, head gardener at the Duke of Devonshire's ancestral home, Chatsworth, in Derbyshire. The elaborate, ribbed, cellular network on the underside of the

ABOVE: *A view down on to the main pool in the Princess of Wales Conservatory shows variation in shape and form of the leaves of some tropical aquatic plants. The most conspicuous are the huge circular leaves – up to 2 metres (6 feet) across – of the giant waterlily, named in honour of Queen Victoria. Living in steamy backwaters of the River Amazon, each leaf is buoyed up so well by a network of strong veins beneath that it can support the weight of a small child.*

Giant waterlily, Victoria 'Longwood
hybrid'
Princess of Wales Conservatory
15 June 1989

ABOVE: *Water lettuce floats as open rosettes on water in tropical and subtropical regions. The plants sold by British garden centres for stocking outdoor ponds will not survive the winter if left outside. In the wild, water lettuce increases so rapidly that it soon carpets open water and cuts out the light below. At Kew, it shares a pool with ornamental koi carp.*

Koi carp surfaces among water lettuce,
 Pistia stratiotes
Princess of Wales Conservatory
15 June 1989

huge leaves provide both strength and buoyancy. It was this design that gave Paxton the inspiration for his structural model of the roof support for the Crystal Palace, designed by him to house the 1851 Great Exhibition.

The first glasshouse in which the giant waterlily was grown at Kew turned out to be too small, so the Waterlily House was built specially for it in 1852. Designed by Richard Turner, who assisted with the design of the Palm House (see p.46), it is sited at the north end of the Palm House. When the giant waterlily was introduced to the Princess of Wales Conservatory, smaller tropical lilies including the sacred lotus, *Nelumbo nucifera*, could be grown in the Waterlily House.

Nowadays a hybrid giant waterlily, *Victoria* 'Longwood Hybrid', made originally at Longwood Gardens in the USA, is treated as an annual, being grown each year from seed. It is planted out in a submerged tub in the main pool of the Princess of Wales Conservatory. Once several leaves have developed, growth is rapid and flowers begin to form. These are white on first opening, but by the following day they have turned a deep pink colour. Many countries, including India, Singapore, Italy, Germany and Hawaii, have grown giant waterlily plants from Kew material. Usually seeds are distributed in vials of water, but sometimes seedlings are dispatched.

Emerging through the surface of the giant waterlily pool are tall clumps of graceful papyrus, *Cyperus papyrus*, with their large open mop-heads. Thousands of years ago the Egyptians used the pithy insides of papyrus stems to make their scrolls. The plant is still used in Ethiopia today to make boats, and the adventurer Thor Heyerdahl had his boat *Ra* made from papyrus stems to prove his theory that Ancient Egyptians could have reached the Americas thousands of years before Columbus.

Tropical plants that share the giant waterlily pool include tropical waterlilies, *Nymphaea caerulea*, and water lettuce, *Pistia stratiotes*. Although diminutive in size compared with the giant waterlily, *Pistia* plants – which resemble miniature floating cabbages – quickly invade open water to form a light green carpet. *Pistia* also shares a smaller pool with colourful koi carp in the bromeliads section, reached from the larger pool by walking through the underpass. Another invasive tropical floating plant found in this pool is the water hyacinth, with a bulbous base to each leaf filled with spongy tissue that buoys up the plant. Water hyacinth is notorious as a noxious weed, choking waterways in Egypt, India, Malaysia, the southern part of the United States and parts of Australia, but it is important in water purification work and it may prove invaluable as a medium for future biogas production (see p.15).

Growing at the water's edge of a smaller pool are plants from mangrove swamps that require a waterlogged soil. Among the mangroves here are several attractive crinum lilies, including *Crinum moorei*, from South Africa and the Mexican *C. cruentum*, bearing long-stalked red stamens, as well as the leather fern, *Acrostichum aureum*, which is widespread in the tropics.

Adjacent to the giant waterlily pool is a small, cooler area planted entirely with carnivorous plants, many of which frequent boggy ground. Here can be seen a variety of sundews, pitcher plants, butterworts and the Venus flytrap, all of which lure their prey by nectar secretions.

Whatever shape their leaves – circular, oval or spathulate – sundews, *Drosera* spp., are covered with glandular hairs that secrete a sticky substance from their tips. Invariably bright red in colour, the tentacle-like hairs function as super-efficient flypaper. When sundews are lit from behind by the sun, each glandular hair glistens like a dew drop in the sun. Around the margins of the leaf, the glandular hairs have longer stalks, while those near the centre of the leaf are shorter and secrete digestive enzymes. Attracted by nectar secretions of the hairs, an insect either crawls up or alights on the leaves, thereby becoming enmeshed. As it struggles to escape, the hairs on the leaf margins begin to bend over, pressing the insect down onto the centre of the leaf.

Sundews have a worldwide distribution and they range in size from a North American species on the Gulf Coast, *D. filiformis* var. *tracyi*, which produces leaves up to 50 centimetres (20 inches) long, to minute pygmy sundews a few millimetres high. The latter grow in south-west Australia, an area which carries the greatest concentration of *Drosera* species in the world. Here they grow in dry ground where they remain dormant until the rains fall.

The Venus flytrap, *Dionaea muscipula*, has an even more spectacular means of ensnaring its prey, for each leaf is modified into a bi-lobed spring trap reminiscent of miniature mantraps. Each lobe has three colourless hairs on the centre and some fifteen to twenty conspicuous teeth along the edge. When an insect lands on the leaves and touches more than one hair or a single hair twice, the leaves snap together, trapping the prey. As the two lobes press tightly together, so enzymes are produced to digest the insect.

Pitcher plants adopt another variation on the theme for trapping their prey. Instead of moving tentacles or closing traps, they rely on the structure of their pitcher making it impossible for any hapless insect which falls in to climb out to safety away from the liquid grave. The body of a drowned insect is then quickly broken down by digestive enzymes secreted by the pitcher. In the United States of America, pitchers such as *Sarracenia* and *Darlingtonia californica* grow directly on the ground in boggy conditions; whereas Old World pitchers, such as *Nepenthes* spp., scramble over vegetation in humid jungles,

RIGHT: *Crinum lilies are large bulbous plants which occur in warm and tropical parts of both the Old and New World. They produce striking white or nearly white flowers arranged in umbels.*

A crinum lily, Crinum cruentum
Princess of Wales Conservatory, Wet Tropics section
27 June 1991

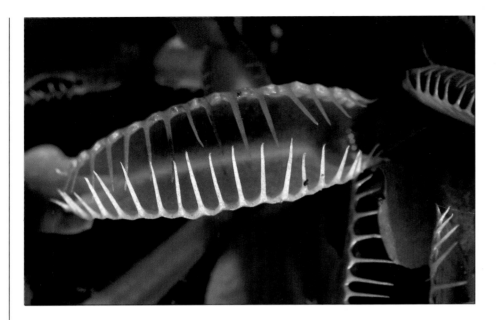

LEFT: *Of all the devices used by carnivorous plants to capture their prey, the sudden snapping together of the bi-lobed spring of the Venus flytrap is the most spectacular. Once caught, the body of the hapless insect is then broken down by the plant's enzymes.*

Venus flytrap, Dionaea muscipula
Princess of Wales Conservatory, Carnivorous Plant display
8 November 1991

with their living traps dangling on the end of stalks. The latter can be found in the main section of the Princess of Wales Conservatory against a wall opposite the giant waterlily pool in the Wet Tropics section.

Before this conservatory was opened, tropical freshwater aquatics were grown in aquatic benches in which the plants were viewed from above. This worked well for observing floating plants, but it proved almost impossible to see the structure of submerged leaves and stems. Now, housed in a series of tanks set into a wall of the underpass in the new Conservatory, they are lit by overhead lighting and can be appreciated to the full.

The Marine Display is also housed in tanks — much larger in size — located in the basement of the Palm House. As you descend the spiral staircase you leave behind the tropical rainforest environment and enter a kaleidoscopic world of mobile colours associated with tropical coral reefs. Like tropical rainforests, these are also habitats with a rich and varied range of species, so it is appropriate that they should both be given star billing at Kew.

When the Palm House was restored in the 1980s, before new planting beds were made in the north and south ends, the basements had to be completely rebuilt. It was then decided to excavate the entire area below the centre transept to house a Marine Display specifically for showing marine algae. The significance of algae to life in general is perhaps best appreciated by the quotation from Sir David Attenborough which appears at the bottom of the stairs leading up from the Marine Display: 'Without algae there would be no life on Earth, the oceans would be sterile and the land uncolonized'.

Five of the nineteen tanks in the display depict British marine habitats, while the remainder are tropical. Two of the British exhibits are tidal: the rocky shore and the salt marsh. In the rocky shore tank, high-tide conditions occur daily from 11 a.m. to 2 p.m., and then from 2 to 4.30 p.m. the water level drops to simulate the tide ebbing down the shore. The salt marsh will most likely be exposed to the air, for it is inundated by a high spring tide only once a fortnight. Of the other two larger tanks, one depicts life in a rock pool and the other houses large brown seaweeds known as kelps. A smaller tank displays sea grasses, *Zostera* spp., the food of Brent geese which migrate south to overwinter in British estuaries. These grasses, when dried, were once used for stuffing mattresses.

However, the most popular attractions are, without doubt, the tanks depicting life in tropical waters, notably on coral reefs. In addition to plant life, these tanks contain fish and marine invertebrates, including sea anemones, clams, sea cucumbers and sea urchins. Marine algae come in a variety of colours – blue-green, green, red and brown. The tropical tanks have been planted so as to provide examples of the various kinds of algae living in different oceans. Thus plants of a sandy lagoon in the Caribbean are located in a separate tank from plants of a sandy lagoon in the Great Barrier Reef; as are tropical brown algae, tropical green algae and tropical deepwater red algae.

Mention has already been made of the way in which long red wavelengths of light are quickly absorbed by seawater. Green algae live in shallow water where they can utilize the red light; somewhat deeper down, brown algae absorb blue-green light; while red algae, able to utilize short blue wavelengths, grow at the deepest depth of any marine plants. The lights over the red algae tanks are therefore switched off during part of each day, so that they are lit for a total of only seven to nine hours in twenty-four.

BELOW: *Sundews are insectivorous plants which trap their prey by means of leaves covered with sticky tentacles. A sweet substance attracts insects and, as one attempts to break free from the sticky snare, the tentacles are stimulated to bend over the victim. Digestive enzymes secreted by the plant break down the insect's body, so that nitrogenous substances can be absorbed.*

Fork-leaved sundew, Drosera binata
Princess of Wales Conservatory, Carnivorous Plant display
6 July 1989

LEFT: *A microcosm within one of the tropical tanks in the Marine Display shows a green alga above an encrusting red coralline alga and brown coral polyps.*

Tropical algae with coral polyps Marine Display, Palm House 18 May 1991

RIGHT: *A variety of invertebrate animals, including sea urchins, can be seen in one of the tropical tanks housed in the Palm House basement. Urchins use their mass of suckered feet (podia) to grip on to vertical or overhead surfaces. This underview shows the blue suckers with the five central teeth used to rasp away at algae.*

Underside of tropical sea urchin Marine Display, Palm House 18 May 1991

Two tropical tanks show the plant life at the top of the shore. Like the British salt marsh, the mangrove swamp is tidal. Amphibious fish known as mudskippers haul themselves out on the mud banks, each defending its own territory. The other tank depicts beach flora high up a tropical shore, with plants such as beach morning glory, *Ipomaea pes-caprae*.

The tidal cycle, the light levels and the water temperature of each tank are controlled by time switches. For corals to survive, all the tropical tanks must be maintained above 20°C (68°F), while the brown seaweeds found around British shores will die if kept in water above 13°C (55.4°F). The artificial seawater cannot be circulated indefinitely, so every month one tenth is drained and replaced.

On display in the Caribbean sandy lagoon tank is a tropical green alga, *Caulerpa taxifolia*, which has been kept in tropical aquaria at the Oceanographic Museum, Monaco for some fifteen years. After being accidentally introduced to the sea below the aquarium in 1984, it survived winter temperatures down to 11°C (51.8°F). Since then it has spread rapidly, being able to reproduce by both sexual and vegetative means. This alga contains the toxin caulerpenyn, which can accumulate in fish browsers such as the Mediterranean bream, *Sarpa salpa*, rendering them unsuitable for human consumption. This accidental introduction highlights the need for stricter control over the release of exotic species into the wild.

Wetlands are certainly not wastelands. Rivers are especially important in that they link land with the sea. Freshwater aquatic plants the world over are under threat as land is drained for agriculture or building development, and the water table is lowered as ground water is extracted for drinking and irrigation. Housing, as well as industrial development, can lead to further

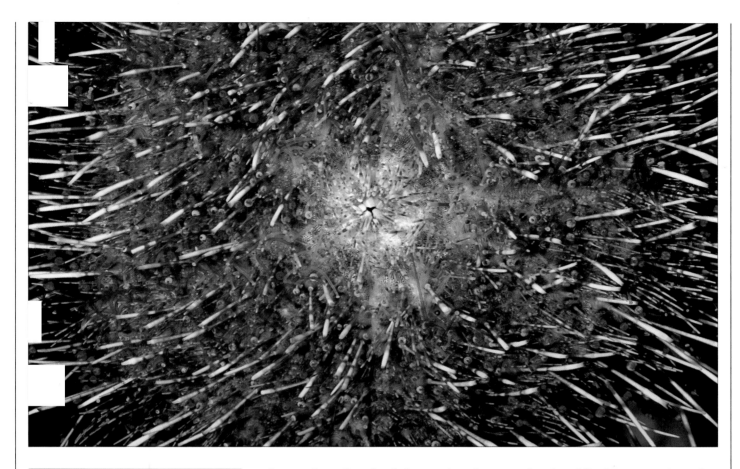

ABOVE: *Once established in a tank, a pearly jawfish soon develops its own territory with a burrow into which it can escape. Here it shares a tank with a tropical green alga,* Udotea flabellum.

Pearly jawfish, Opistognathus *sp. with alga,* Udotea flabellum
Marine Display, Palm House
20 May 1991

destruction of wetlands by causing the water level to fall when water is used at a faster rate than it accumulates. The construction of huge dam projects in tropical countries has altered the flow rate of rivers and also reduced wetland sites. More recently, acid rain has had a devastating impact on lakes in the United States, Canada and Europe.

The intensive use of nitrogenous fertilizers for agriculture results in increased nitrate levels in freshwater systems as polluted water runs off the land and enters streams and rivers. Nitrates, together with phosphates, are the major cause of the eutrophication of lakes and rivers which occurs when plant plankton grows so rapidly that it outstrips the grazers which normally control its abundance. As the plankton dies and decays, so the oxygen levels in the water are depleted, resulting in the death of many other inhabitants.

Wild waterlilies may not produce such large or colourful blooms as the cultivars now sold at aquatic centres, but their flowers are just as exquisite. Sadly waterlilies are declining, because their habitats are being destroyed. Taking the British Isles as an example, a 1988 survey showed that the white waterlily, *Nymphaea alba*, which was plentiful in rivers as well as the Norfolk Broads during the last century, now occurs in only 5 per cent of its former localities. Indeed, proof of the lush aquatic vegetation that once flourished on the Broads can be seen in an 1887 photograph by P.H. Emerson. Entitled 'Gathering water-lilies' it depicts a couple in a rowing boat, the man slowly guiding the craft so that the lady can gather a flower. Motor boats are one of the main reasons for the demise of the white waterlily on the Broads, and this attractive plant is now confined to a few quiet backwaters where motor boats are prohibited. Pollution, especially high nitrogen levels in the water, is another detrimental factor and illegal collecting of the plants does not help.

Marine algae are also threatened by pollution, chiefly by large oil slicks, which cut out light – an essential factor for photosynthesis to take place. Coral reefs, with their associated algae, invertebrates and fish, are extremely rich ecosystems. However, if they are polluted by sewage or pesticides, or if the coral polyps are smothered by silt washed down from the land, many species die and their diversity is catastrophically reduced.

Along more sheltered tropical shores and lagoons, mangroves thrive. Their interwoven roots trap silt and function as a natural defence against the impact of stormy seas on the shore. Once mangroves are damaged or destroyed, erosion inevitably follows.

Moving water plays a major part in the dispersal of aquatic plants by transporting not only floating seeds and fruits but also vegetative parts including floating stems and bulbils. Some plants, such as rushes, *Juncus* spp., and the monkey flower, *Mimulus* spp., produce seeds that are denser than water, so they sink. After germination, their seedlings bob up to the surface where they are dispersed by water currents. If they become trapped in tree roots or other bankside debris, they can then take root.

Floating aquatics, such as duckweeds, *Lemna* spp., water ferns, *Azolla* spp., and water lettuce, can be dispersed by flooding and also by animals visiting ponds and pools to drink or breed. In Zambia, I have seen a hippopotamus emerge from a pool covered with water lettuce and transport several plants on its back along dusty tracks to another enclosed pool.

In still, warm water, *Azolla* grows quickly; indeed, during hot summers at Kew, a complete barrow-load is removed each week from just one pool in the Aquatic Garden. A few plants of *Azolla* are an attractive addition to any temperate aquarium or garden pool, but when they multiply and carpet the entire surface, they inevitably have to be thinned out. The obvious solution might seem to be to dispose of them in the wild; however, such an apparently innocuous action can have far-reaching effects. In 1888, a teacher brought some *Azolla filiculoides* all the way from Glasgow to Norfolk, disposing of the plantlets in a ditch near the River Bure. Heavy floods during August 1912 transported the *Azolla* up the Bure, Thurne and Ant rivers. A preferable means of disposal is to skim off the *Azolla* plants and use them as a nitrogen-rich fertilizer. As moorhens and other waterfowl swim amongst *Azolla* carpets, plantlets accidentally caught up in their feathers can be relocated elsewhere. Duckweeds are carried on birds' feet, while amphibious newts, frogs and toads inadvertently transport duckweed on their backs as they leave their breeding pools and move overland to other water bodies.

Until recently the exquisite beauty of marine algae living below the tides could be appreciated only by scuba divers; but now Kew's Marine Display enables any visitor to gain some insight into the diversity of plant life under the sea. Just as terrestrial plants provide shelter and nourishment for some land animals, so algae provide cover for fish and other marine organisms, food for grazers and an anchorage point for more sedentary fish.

Now that the multifarious problems associated with displaying marine algae, from both temperate and tropical seas, have been overcome, it would be interesting to see yet another innovative exhibit of aquatic plants at Kew. The structure of submerged aquatics living in constantly flowing freshwater could perhaps be observed through a glass-sided tank. Like the marine tanks, this would not only add to the enjoyment and education of visitors, but would also provide a new dimension for botanists researching aquatic plants, including perhaps some species that have proved to be particularly invasive.

ABOVE: *During the summer, the floating fern,* Azolla, *proliferates so quickly that the raised pools in the corners of the Aquatic Garden become covered with a green carpet tinged with pink. A native of western North America,* Azolla *cannot survive harsh winters outside.*

An aquatic fern, Azolla filiculoides
Aquatic Garden
12 April 1991

RIGHT: *The new leaves of the variegated form of yellow flag are especially attractive when the sun shines through them. By late summer, the leaves are uniformly green. Nestling against the upright iris plants are pink clumps of the aquatic fern,* Azolla.

Iris pseudacorus *'Variegata' with* Azolla
Aquatic Garden
28 April 1991

CHAPTER FIVE

DESERT PLANTS

Able to survive an irregular water supply and temperatures that range from the searing heat of midday to well below freezing at night, desert plants show some of the most extraordinary adaptations of any plants on earth. Kew's exhibits of desert plants span the globe from Arizona and Mexico to the Namib Desert, from the sands of Arabia to Madagascar.

THE RANGE OF plants able to survive the inhospitable desert landscape may be small compared with the rich rainforest flora, but their interest lies in the multifarious ways in which they have adapted to survive not only a sparse and irregular supply of water, but also a huge diurnal temperature range. Deserts receive less than 25 centimetres (10 inches) of rain per year and occur between latitudes 20° and 30° north and south of the Equator. They are also found along fogbound coastal strips of Peru and Namibia and in rain shadow areas on the lee of mountain ranges, such as the Patagonian Desert adjacent to the Andes. More than a fifth of the world's land surface is covered by desert and semi-desert, by no means all of which is shifting sand dunes. Rocks or boulders may litter sandy or gravelly plains or alkaline flats and, after huge temporary lakes evaporate, the ground cracks open into the typical polygonal stress patterns which develop when fine sediments dry out.

The Sahara, spanning the northern part of the African continent and stretching from the Atlantic coast to the Red Sea and on into Asia, is the largest single desert. Further south is the Kalahari Desert in Botswana and,

LEFT: *A good rain late in the year on deserts in the south-west of the United States triggers a spectacular flowering the following spring. Here in Organ Pipe National Monument, Arizona, a hedgehog cactus,* Echinocereus engelmanii, *flowers among a golden carpet of brittlebush,* Encelis farinosa, *in March.*

to the west of this, the Namib Desert in South West Africa. This coastal desert strip receives less than 20 millimetres ($\frac{3}{4}$ inch) annually of rain, but coastal fog and extensive early-morning dew provide enough additional moisture for several unusual plants to grow, none more so than *Welwitschia mirabilis* with its pair of wide, strap-shaped, opposite leaves, their ends frayed by constant rubbing against the sand. If one of the leaves is lost, the plant will die. Unlike many desert plants that show a reduction in the number of microscopic pores or stomata on their leaves, *Welwitschia* has more per square millimetre (some 250) than almost any other plant, temperate or tropical.

Named in honour of the Austrian naturalist Friedrich Martin Josef Welwitsch, who discovered it in 1859, this bizarre plant is classed within the gymnosperms (together with cycads, the ginkgo and conifers). Male and female cones develop on branching sprays on separate plants; pollen carried by the wind becomes trapped on the sticky surface of the female cones. The pollen grains germinate and form a pollen tube but, unlike any other plant,

BELOW: *At the southern entrance to the Princess of Wales Conservatory, some of the plants in North America's Mojave Desert have been planted in a special display with a diorama painted behind. Among them are several* Ferocactus *and* Opuntia *cacti as well as agaves, nolinias and yuccas, including a small joshua tree,* Yucca brevifolia.

Sherman Hoyt diorama of the Mojave Desert Princess of Wales Conservatory, Dry Tropics section
12 May 1991

RIGHT: *Welwitschia is undoubtedly an oddity of the plant world, bearing just a pair of strap-shaped leaves. It lives only in the Namib Desert of south-west Africa, where the rainfall is scanty but the plants are bathed in heavy early morning dews and sea mists. Separate male and female plants produce cones on branches arising between the leaves.*

Welwitschia mirabilis
Princess of Wales Conservatory, Wet Tropics section
14 January 1992

the egg travels up the pollen tube instead of the male cell passing down to the egg. Several *Welwitschia* plants can be seen at Kew in an alcove leading off the Wet Tropics section of the Princess of Wales Conservatory, only one of which, a male, has so far produced cones.

At one time succulents and cacti were temporarily planted outdoors during the summer in a bed near the Rock Garden, proving that many of these plants will survive a British summer. Now an extensive permanent display can be seen in the Dry Tropics section at the southern end of the Princess of Wales Conservatory, with May being the peak month for cacti flowers. The gulley running through the main planting area separates New World cacti and succulents (opuntias, agaves, yuccas and nolinias) from Old World plants such as aloes and euphorbias. A few montane desert cacti can be seen in the south-east corner of the Alpine House. Within the Conservatory are plants from Namibia, Madagascar, South Africa, Mexico, the southern USA and Arabia, but there are none from the Gobi Desert. Australian desert flora is also lacking, because it has adapted in a different way from that of flora from other desert regions. In Australian deserts, instead of cacti and succulents, there are trees and shrubs with tiny, short-lived leaves which are lost as drought conditions prevail, new ones appearing when the rains come; other shrubs bear leaves that wither, but revive on wetting. Heavy rain also triggers the germination of dormant seeds of annuals, resulting in ephemeral floral carpets.

A variety of adaptations enables the perennial desert plants to survive the harsh conditions of searing heat by day and plummeting temperatures at night, coupled with scanty, irregular rainfall. Conservation of what little water is present is overcome by modification of leaves into spines and storage of water inside the plant, as well as the shedding of leaves during the dry season. The coachwhip or ocotillo, *Fouquieria splendens*, endemic to Mexico and the southern USA, stands with leafless, wand-like stems for most of the year; but since these contain chlorophyll, they can take on the role of photosynthesis normally carried out by the leaves. Rain triggers the leaves to sprout anew and, in years when intermittent rains fall, several periods of foliation and defoliation occur.

Even though cacti are synonymous with deserts, they are not confined to these habitats; they also occur high up mountains and as rainforest epiphytes. Nearly all cacti have solved the problem of conserving water by modifying their leaves into dry spines and having a viscid sap containing mucilage. The

Defence in desert plants comes in a variety of shapes and colours. The golden barrel cactus has simple golden spines, agaves and furcraeas have prickles along the leaf margins, and the horse crippler has dagger-like spines on the prostrate stems.

LEFT: *Golden barrel cactus,* Echino-cactus grusonii
14 January 1992

TOP RIGHT: *Variegated furcraea,* Furcraea selloana
22 December 1991

BOTTOM RIGHT: *Horse crippler or creeping devil,* Machaerocereus eruca
22 December 1991

Princess of Wales Conservatory, Dry Tropics section

spines of most cacti are simple and straight, but they may be hooked (as in fishhook cacti) or even barbed (as in glochids on *Opuntia* cacti, whose spines can be quite painful and irritating when they penetrate the skin). Hooked spines on the smaller *Mammillaria* aid dispersal as their offsets become entangled in the fur or feathers of passing animals. Spines are also well developed in the Didierea family from Madagascar, and are interspersed among small, flat, ephemeral leaves shed during the dry season. The long spines on *Pelargonium spinosum* and *P. crassicaule* develop from leaf stalks after the blade drops. Prickles, another type of armament found on desert plants, can be seen at Kew on *Euphorbia millii* in the Madagascar collection and along the margins of *Agave* leaves in the Mexican collection.

The beard cacti, notably the old man cactus, *Cephalocereus senilis*, is covered with a mat of fine white hairs that reduces water loss by reflecting bright light and by trapping air. *Espostoa* cacti of high-altitude Andean deserts

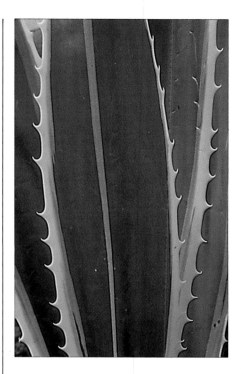

also have a covering of thin, white, hair-like spines which serve both to reflect light and as thermo-regulators. The air trapped by day keeps the cactus warm during the chill night, while the air trapped at night keeps it cool in the intense daytime heat.

Competition for space in the desert occurs underground. The typical sparse and widely spaced desert vegetation is fed by such extensive root systems that, if they were all unearthed and upended, the ground would appear as completely covered as a tropical rainforest! Such root systems enable desert plants to maximize water uptake when rain does come. Three distinct types of roots occur: a wide-ranging lateral development (as in most cacti), a big vertical tap root (as in the joint fir, *Ephedra* sp., and night-blooming cereus, *Cereus greggii*) and a combination of both side roots and a tap root (as in the creosote bush, *Larrea tridentata*). In places such as the Sonoran Desert, where creosote bushes are abundant, they are spaced out equidistantly from one another as a result of a chemical produced by the roots inhibiting the growth of seedlings which begin to germinate nearby.

Succulents store water in their stems, leaves or roots. Nearly all cacti are succulent, but by no means all succulents are cacti. Leaf succulents such as *Crassula* and *Echeveria*, as well as stone plants, *Lithops* and *Conophytum*, store water in their fleshy leaves, while stem succulents such as *Euphorbia, Opuntia,*

LEFT: Echeveria *is a genus of succulents found from Texas to Argentina, with the majority in Mexico. The radially symmetrical leaf rosettes of some species have been prized as summer bedding plants, notably for floral clocks, since Victorian times. They can be cultivated by seed or from a single leaf.*

Echeveria umbricata
Nursery
8 November 1991

RIGHT: *Both the grey colour and the arrangement of the spines into double-edged combs give this Mexican cactus a resemblance to rows of woodlice. As it is very slow-growing, it is sometimes grafted on to more vigorous tissue to encourage faster growth. The rosy-purple flowers are surrounded by woolly hairs.*

Woodlouse or hatchet cactus,
  Pelecyphora aselliformis
Nursery
22 December 1991

Stapelia and *Kleinia* use this part of the plant not only to store water but also for photosynthesis. Root succulents such as the peyote, *Lophophora williamsii*, from Mexico and Texas develop a huge, fleshy tap root which functions as an underground food and water store. But it is the spineless, green 'buttons', which appear above ground, that are sought after by Mexican Indians. Long before the drug LSD (lysergic acid diethylamide) hit the headlines in the world press, the Indians were using the dried 'buttons' to produce hallucinations during their religious rituals. Known also as the LSD cactus, the peyote contains many drug substances and it has long been illegal to sell this plant on the open market in North America.

Many euphorbias, notably *Euphorbia horrida* from South Africa, look remarkably cactus-like, with a succulent stem and spines, but all spiny euphorbias can be distinguished from cacti in that their spines emerge in pairs from a hard spine shield, whereas cacti have five or more spines emerging from a felted cushion known as an areole.

There are also succulents in families which are typically non-succulent such as kleinias (daisy family), the desert rose, *Adenium obesum* (periwinkle family), *Cissus* (vine family) and *Dorstenia* (mulberry family). Dorstenias, such as *D. foetida* from southern Arabia, develop a curious inflorescence with small flowers (and later fruit) embedded in a flat, green receptacle bordered by long tentacles. The seeds are shot out explosively, by differential contraction, over a distance of up to 6 metres ($19\frac{1}{2}$ feet) from the parent plant. A lush, leafy relative, *D. bahiensis* from Brazil – grown in the Wet Tropics section of the Princess of Wales Conservatory – bears a similar type of inflorescence.

Good water storage is not enough to ensure survival; water must be used as economically as possible. Plants which live in much less extreme places than deserts, with a higher and more even distribution of rain, photosynthesize by day, taking in carbon dioxide and losing water vapour via the stomata in their leaves. During drought periods, when the loss of water exceeds the uptake, such plants will wilt. Cacti, members of the stonecrop family (Crassulaceae)

ABOVE: *Spines occur only on young peyote seedlings, but on the mature plant they are replaced by tufts of felted hairs. An overhead view of a peyote shows an unusual pattern of these felted tufts; more typically they are arranged in straight, rather than spiral, lines.*

Peyote or mescal, Lophophora williamsii
Nursery
22 December 1991

LEFT: *Melocactus grows for some ten years without flowering, then a top-knot — known as a cephalium — develops. At this stage, the cactus ceases to grow and small pinkish flowers appear through the hairs and bristles. Found in Mexico, tropical South America and the West Indies, melocactus was among the first cacti to be brought to Europe.*

Turk's cap, Melocactus bellavistensis,
  with cephalium
Nursery
8 November 1991

and some other succulents reduce water loss by closing their stomata by day and opening them at night when the air is cool and evaporation is much lower. But these plants still have to photosynthesize in daylight and they do so by utilizing carbon dioxide taken in through the stomata at night and temporarily converted to acids.

Water is also lost when a flower opens, so small flowers of desert plants may open for a limited time only, while large flowers, such as the cream blooms on the gigantic Mexican cardon, *Pachycereus pringlei*, open in late evening when the temperature has dropped. Flowers of the columnar saguaro cactus, *Carnegia gigantea* — familiar from cowboy films — are, however, more numerous on the east side of the stem. Queen of the night, *Selenicereus grandiflorus*, is also a night bloomer, but the huge flowers close early the next day. A cereus at Kew has repeatedly produced large flowers at night, although by the time visitors arrive in the morning, the flowers have normally wilted. In the desert, jumping cholla cactus, *Opuntia fulgida*, flowers have such a precise opening time that it is possible to set a watch by them — around 3 p.m. on a sunny day and 2.30 p.m. on a cloudy day.

RIGHT: *A succession of attractive velvet crimson flowers is produced by this Bolivian cactus over a period of several months at Kew. The tubular flowers, which open by day, arise from the columnar, deeply-ribbed stems.*

Cleistocactus samaipatanus
*Princess of Wales Conservatory, Dry Tropics
  section*
12 June 1991

LEFT: *A pane had to be removed from the glass roof of the Conservatory to allow the flowering spike of this agave from Mexico to develop fully. As the sap surges up to feed the developing spike, so the leaves begin to die; by the time the seed ripens, the leaves are completely shrivelled.*

Agave franzosinii
Princess of Wales Conservatory, Dry Tropics section
9 August 1991

Another strategy for survival, adopted by desert annuals, is to telescope their lifespan into a few brief weeks, after which seeds lie dormant until the rain falls. Rain transforms a desert. As water drains off sandy flats, dry washes become raging temporary rivers. A light shower or a fall of dew will not be sufficient to trigger germination of seeds of annuals and other desert plants containing a germination inhibitor; a heavy soaking from prolonged rain is required to wash out the inhibitor before the seeds can germinate. This is why landmark years, when deserts become ablaze with flowers, are few and far between. In the Sonoran Desert, which stretches south from southern California and Arizona into Mexico, golden *Eschscholzia* poppies and purple

ABOVE: *The beard cacti from the high-altitude deserts of the Andes are covered with a fine wool-like mat of hairs. This protects the plant from the temperature extremes which range from 20°C at midday to −5°C at night.*

Beard cactus, Espostoa lanata
Princess of Wales Conservatory, Dry Tropics section
14 January 1992

owl clover, *Orthocarpus purpurescens,* both produce colourful carpets among the cacti. On the other hand, in South Africa's Namaqualand, it is the daisies that put on the most spectacular shows: as they unfurl their petals, the entire ground seems to turn yellow, orange or white. Many of these plants are familiar to gardeners the world over – annuals such as dimorphothecas, arctotis, cotulas and osteospermums and perennials such as gazanias and arcothecas. To experience the transformation of these desert landscapes from utter drabness to a bejewelled wonderland is unforgettable. Sadly such a glory cannot be recreated within the limited area under glass.

Among the largest desert plants on display at Kew are the Old World tree-like aloes and the New World agaves with their huge leaf rosettes up to 3 metres (10 feet) across and flowering stems so tall that glass panes in the Conservatory have to be removed in summer. When agaves were grown in tubs in the Orangery, their flowering spikes had to be beheaded before they reached and damaged the ceiling.

Agaves are striking evergreen perennial plants of arid and semi-arid parts of sub-tropical and tropical regions of the Americas. The leaves grow for many years – although not for as long as a century, as was mistakenly believed of the century plant, *Agave americana* – before the flower spike develops. The energy needed for the production of agave flower spikes comes from food stored in the leaves which gradually shrivel so that the plants flower only once before they die. In Mexico the huge surge of sap that rises up the developing flower stem is collected by removal of the young flower head. The fermented juice, *pulque,* is a national drink and when distilled produces the spirit *tequila.*

In warmer climates larger agaves are often used in gardens as living architectural features, planted in urns or in pairs on either side at the top of flights of steps. *A. americana* is now naturalized along the Mediterranean coast and *A. americana* 'Marginata', with a yellow border to the green leaves, is a popular variety grown outdoors in Britain, where it needs to be protected during the winter. The leaves of *A. sisalana* and *A. fourcroydes,* both natives of Central America, yield the tough fibres used for rope making, known respectively as sisal and henequen. Sisal is produced from commercial plantations in Brazil, Madagascar and east Africa.

Yuccas are another group of plants from Mexico and the southern USA grown at Kew. At first glance they resemble smaller versions of agaves, but closer inspection reveals that they have more leaves, looser in bud, the outer ones not leaving an impression on the younger inner ones as in many agaves. While most yuccas are grown inside the Princess of Wales Conservatory, hardier kinds can be seen outside at the southern end. Yuccas produce creamy flowers which are pollinated in the wild by the yucca moth, *Pronuba yuccasella.* After collecting pollen, the female moth moulds it into balls which she stuffs into the cupped stigmas of other yucca flowers she visits (thereby unwittingly ensuring cross-pollination) and lays one or two eggs on each ovary. When the caterpillars hatch they feed on some of the developing ovaries, but leave others to mature fully into seeds. Here is a case of complete interdependence of a plant and an insect, proved by the fact that when yuccas are cultivated in places outside the moths' range, no seeds develop unless the flowers are pollinated by hand.

Euphorbias comprise a vast group of succulents which shows great diversity of form, ranging from the tiny, ground-hugging *Euphorbia albo-marginata,* found in California's Death Valley, to trees such as *E. tetragona,* from South Africa, reaching over 12 metres (40 feet) high. When the leaves or stems of euphorbias are cut, they exude a milky latex which is poisonous to animals and can cause severe allergic skin reactions in some people. The latex from *E. tiracelli* is used as a fish poison in Kenya: when it is added to small ponds, the affected fish float to the surface where they can be caught; any latex on the skin is wiped off before the fish is cooked and eaten. Euphorbia flowers are unusual, each bearing a single female flower surrounded by several male flowers and larger bracts, the whole referred to as a cyathium.

Stapelias or carrion flowers are a group of succulents from tropical and southern parts of Africa which produce foetid-smelling, reddish-brown or purple (often blotched with yellow) flowers to attract their pollinators. Flies, lured by the smell of rotting meat or fish emitted by these blooms, home in on them and accidentally pick up the sticky pollen on their hairy legs or pro-boscis as they move around to feed. The thick, almost leathery petals lose little water and remain open for several days. Carrion flowers belong to the milk-weed family, producing pods inside which are seeds bearing a fine, hairy pappus that aids wind dispersal.

Ceropegias, a related group consisting mainly of succulents and found in Africa, Madagascar and the Canary Islands, also produce malodorous flowers which attract flies. The rosary vine or string of hearts, *C. woodii* ssp. *woodii*, is an attractive trailing pot plant with paired heart-shaped leaves and curious tubular flowers. *C. haygarthi*i from South Africa, also trailing, produces a hairy brush on top of a long stalk above the flower proper. As the flower moves in the wind, the brush becomes a wriggly lure, somewhat reminiscent of that used by angler fish to attract their prey to within reach of their large mouth. Once flies enter the tubular flowers of the plant, they become trapped by the downward-pointing hairs. They crawl out, dusted with pollen, when the hairs wither and cross-pollinate the next flower they visit.

In the South African and Namibian deserts, the leaves of many stone plants such as *Fenestraria*, *Lithops* and *Conophytum* are buried in the ground with just the tops protruding. These have clear 'windows' of translucent tissue – best developed in *Fenestraria* – allowing light to pass through to the green cells

LEFT: *Only when a stone plant bursts into flower does it become conspicuous. For most of the year, the pair of swollen leaves mimic perfectly the surrounding stones and pebbles on South African and Namibian deserts. When a stone plant develops a pair of new leaves at right angles to the old pair, the latter shrivel and die.*

Stone plant, Lithops olivacea
Princess of Wales Conservatory, Dry Tropics section
8 November 1991

below. So well are stone plants camouflaged among the surface pebbles that they are almost impossible to spot – until they burst into bloom.

Madagascar, the world's fourth largest island, which split off from mainland Africa some 100 million years ago, has a high proportion of endemic flora and fauna. In the arid south there are bizarre plants belonging to the Didiereaceae family. *Alluaudia* is like a thick, spinier ocotillo with small, circular leaves that are shed during the dry season. By growing vertically instead of horizontally the leaves cast cooling shadows on the stem.

Cacti do not always reach Kew in prime condition. One sad example was the 100-year-old specimen of *Echinopsis atacamensis* that arrived crammed into a wooden box with most of its roots cut away. Two ropes used to haul the cactus out of the Atacama Desert in Chile had torn into the flesh, leaving obvious rope burns. When one of these developed a rot, diagnosed as bacterial, it was decided to treat the area with Savlon, an antiseptic disinfectant used to treat human bacterial infections. The infected tissue was removed and a solution of 50 per cent Savlon and 50 per cent water applied. By the following morning the oozing had ceased and the wound rapidly healed over, although the scar is still visible.

Most cacti and succulents are routinely propagated at Kew from seed and from stem or leaf tissue. Rarer and more difficult species are propagated by the micro-propagation unit. Smaller cacti and succulents have long attracted the interest of collectors and hobbyists. However, the bright red balls perched atop a green stem sold the world over in markets and florists will not be found at Kew, which is concerned only with the propagation and conservation of true species, not man-made grafts.

But cacti, succulents and other desert flora are more than an unusual assortment of plants that intrigue collectors. Like certain rainforest plants, some desert species provide substances beneficial to man. American Indians have long appreciated their usefulness: for example, when the fruits of the saguaro cactus ripen, they are harvested and the sweet, red pulp inside is used for making syrup, jam and ceremonial wine.

RIGHT: *Yuccas, native to the warmer parts of the United States, are evergreen trees and shrubs belonging to the lily family. This, the variegated form of the Spanish dagger, is one of several striking architectural yuccas bearing a cream flower spike. At Kew, several yuccas and opuntias are protected on two sides by outer glass walls, but further south in Europe, including the French Riviera, they grow well in the open.*

Yucca gloriosa variegata
Outside the Princess of Wales Conservatory
9 September 1991

For centuries the Indians have gathered the nuts of jojoba – pronounced 'ho-ho-ba' – *Simmondsia chinensis*, and crushed the seeds to extract the odourless and colourless liquid wax, which they use for cooking, as a skin cream and even to dress their hair. This plant, which grows naturally in the Sonoran Desert, can be seen with other economic plants in Kew's Temperate House.

Jojoba wax is one of the best skin softeners and is now used as a substitute for many products previously made from sperm whale oil. The plant from which it comes has the advantage of being drought-resistant, living for up to 200 years yet producing fruits after only three to five years. The passing of the 1972 Endangered Species Conservation Act, forbidding the importation of sperm-whale products into the USA, provided the impetus for growing jojoba commercially in North America. It is also cultivated in Israel, India, South Africa, Kenya and Australia. Male and female flowers are produced on separate plants and a ratio of one male to seven females is adopted in commercial plantations. Jojoba oil is now used in engine lubricants, in cosmetics (it facilitates the application of lipstick) and in shampoos.

Aloe vera is another useful desert plant, used by the Ancient Egyptians, Greeks and Romans for medicinal purposes; it is now grown commercially in

Euphorbias are a large and extremely diverse group ranging from exquisite miniatures to huge tree-like forms. Most of the succulent species are African. Like the rubber tree, which is also a member of the spurge family, euphorbias contain a sticky white sap or latex, which causes allergic skin reactions in some people.

ABOVE: *Crown of thorns,* Euphorbia milli *var.* milli *from Madagascar has attractive red bracts around the tiny flowers.*
8 June 1991

TOP LEFT: *Spiral growth of* Euphorbia pugniformis *from Namibia.*
17 September 1991

BOTTOM LEFT: *Details of flowers of* Euphorbia classenii *from Kenya.*
22 December 1991

the southern USA for both cosmetic and medicinal products. The sap is used in sun lotions as a screen against ultra-violet rays and also in preparations to reduce the effects of sunburn. *Opuntia* cacti were cultivated in Mexico, and still are on Lanzarote in the Canary Islands, as the food plant for white scale insects, *Coccus cacti*, from which the red food colouring cochineal is produced.

We hear a great deal about rainforest destruction, but man's activities are extending existing desert areas. This process of desertification occurs naturally as a result of climate change; indeed, we know from cave paintings that only 10,000 years ago parts of the Sahara Desert were green enough to support the wild animals that attract so many tourists to more southerly parts of the African continent today. However, it is the current rate of desertification, brought about as a result of damage to stabilizing vegetation from overgrazing by stock, overcultivation, deforestation or poor irrigation, that is cause for alarm. Land adjacent to all the major desert areas faces the threat of advancing desertification. If this trend is not halted, the pressure on other habitats is put at even greater risk. But low-cost programmes, whereby individuals are encouraged to plant small pockets of trees, can help to stabilize the ground and thereby turn back the deserts. One of the most ambitious projects of this kind has been the planting, over more than a decade, of a Great Green Wall in northern China stretching for 7,000 kilometres (4,350 miles) and extending 400–1,700 kilometres (250–1,055 miles) in width. This was achieved by encouraging people in every township to lend a hand.

For over ten years Kew has been working on a project to aid peoples living in arid and semi-arid regions. In 1981 the development of a database known as SEPASAL (the Survey of Economic Plants for Arid and Semi-arid Lands), a collation of information on useful plants of dryland areas, was initiated at Kew. At first it was funded by OXFAM and then by the Clothworkers' Foundation, but now SEPASAL is funded directly by Kew as part of the work of its Economic and Conservation Section (ECOS). The information has been gathered from many sources, notably the literature contained in the Kew library, from the research laboratories and from first-hand experience of propagating plants from arid and semi-arid regions.

Within these regions, which comprise some 43 per cent of the earth's land surface, plants provide not only shelter and fuel, but also materials for clothing and medicines. The SEPASAL database provides information on the ecology, cultivation, pests and diseases of specific useful plants. It can list by region or soil type or altitude (or any combination of these) the plants that are already in use, and also which ones can be grown in a region where particular questions arise – for example, how a local shortage of cooking oils is to be resolved or which plants are most effective for binding soils together to stop soil erosion. Such information is proving invaluable to organizations as diverse as the World Bank, FAO and OXFAM. These user organizations in turn provide additional information for continually updating SEPASAL. This database is a useful tool in the fight to reverse land degradation – both man-made and natural – resulting from shifts in climate, overgrazing, salinization, and in the aftermath of war and famine.

RIGHT: *The leaf rosettes of the larger agaves are among the most architecturally striking of all the desert plants grown in the Princess of Wales Conservatory. The spiny-edged leaves of agaves – particularly strong in this Mexican species – deter animals from grazing them.*

Agave ferox
Princess of Wales Conservatory, Dry Tropics section
15 May 1992

LEFT: *The Madagascar palm, which lives in a desert region in south-west Madagascar, is a bizarre member of the milkweed family, reminiscent of the famed boojum tree of Baja, California. The thick fleshy column, covered with spines, sports a tuft of strap-like green shining leaves among which funnel-shaped white flowers appear. These are not unlike* Frangipani *flowers.*

Madagascar palm or club foot, Pachypodium lamerei
Princess of Wales Conservatory, Dry Tropics section
17 September 1991

CHAPTER SIX

MONTANE PLANTS

*Montane plants range from tiny,
ground-hugging alpines to the large blooms
of Himalayan rhododendrons. At
Kew, much work has been done to stimulate
the natural habitat of these plants,
in order to extend the range that can be
grown in southern Britain.*

T HERE CAN BE no doubt that montane plants have attracted more interest from the layman than those of any other habitat. Their appeal lies both in their exquisite shape and form and in the thrill experienced in climbing mountains to search for and photograph them. Time spent in the field also naturally enhances knowledge of the terrain and aspect preferred by each particular species, which can be put to good use when growing them in cultivation.

Mention has already been made of the repeated setbacks and dangers faced by Kew collectors travelling to remote parts of the world, and perhaps these were at their worst for those who undertook collecting at altitude. But all the toil, sweat and difficulties involved in climbing high to hunt for plants pale into insignificance when an exquisite flower is sighted growing in the wild for the first time.

Among the problems that beset collectors visiting high elevations was the likelihood of being attacked by unfriendly natives. During his 1835–40 trip to South and Central America, George Barclay was robbed and injured by bandits in the Peruvian Alps. Joseph Hooker, in the course of his 1848–51 explorations to Sikkim, Tibet and East Nepal, was briefly imprisoned in Sikkim at the end of 1849, but he returned with the seed of many spectacular rhododendrons and magnolias. By 1851 he had discovered forty-three

LEFT: *For a few brief weeks in late July and early August, sub-alpine meadows in Canada's Mount Revelstoke National Park in British Columbia are ablaze with colour. The red flowers of Indian paintbrush,* Castilleja miniata, *are the most conspicuous and among them are the tall white-flowered spikes of valerian,* Valeriana sitchensis.

species of rhododendrons in the Sikkim area of the Himalaya and there can be no doubt that it was his introductions that triggered off the enthusiasm for rhododendron collections in Britain. While on location he painted a few flowers and leaves of each species, from which Kew's resident botanical artist could prepare full-colour lithographs.

The Rhododendron Dell at Kew Gardens was originally planted as a Himalayan valley with rhododendrons grown from seed collected by Hooker. Many garden hybrids have resulted from cross-pollination of the original species so that today the Dell contains a mixture of species and hybrid plants. From mid-May to early June is the best time to visit the Rhododendron Dell, but throughout the short winter and early spring days a succession of less hardy montane rhododendrons from the mountains of tropical Malaysia, Indonesia and north China can be enjoyed flowering in the Temperate House. These plants either grow directly in the ground above the treeline as dwarf shrubs or perch as epiphytes in the crowns of trees alongside orchids, mosses and ferns. Most of these rhododendrons were introduced to Britain during this century.

ABOVE: *A variety of exquisite blooms on non-hardy rhododendrons can be seen in the north wing of the Temperate House. Here, the sulphur-yellow, bell-shaped flowers of a New Guinea species are highlighted by sun beaming through the glass behind.*

Rhododendron laetum
Temperate House
26 June 1989

In recent years plant-hunting expeditions from Kew have been made to Afghanistan, Nepal and China in search of specimens for botanical research in the Herbarium and seeds for botanical gardens and possibly for cultivation in the horticultural trade. Even as recently as 1987, when botanists from Kew and Edinburgh Botanic Gardens participated in a joint British-Chinese Expedition to the Lijiang Mountains in Yunnan Province, China, they were not permitted to camp and so had to retrace their steps, sometimes climbing 2,000 metres (6,560 feet) and back again in a single day.

By no means all plants growing high up mountains are small and compact, as the opening picture to this chapter proves. It can be misleading to describe montane plants simply as 'alpines' since this word has different connotations to different people. Horticulturalists use the term to embrace small or slow-growing plants which can be grown outside or in an alpine house; to botanists, the term 'alpine plants' means those that grow in a zone between the upper tree limit and the beginning of permanent snow cover. On both temperate and tropical mountains, alpines occur above the tree line, but in the Arctic, where trees peter out, they grow down to sea level.

Even though rock gardening became popular in Britain during the period 1860–80, only a small area of the mound covering the ice house at Kew displayed such plants at this time. Interestingly enough, Joseph Banks had contributed to the first rock garden constructed in England at the Chelsea Physic Garden, as early as 1771–2. Shortly after William Forsyth had been appointed Gardener at Chelsea, he bought 40 tonnes of old stonework from the Tower of London to create his artificial rock garden. Banks' contribution consisted of pieces of volcanic lava from Iceland which had been brought back to England as ship's ballast. It was more than a century later that George Curling Joad, an admirer of Kew, bequeathed 2,630 alpine and herbaceous plants to the Gardens on condition that they were conveyed to their new home at once. This gesture provided the impetus for the Treasury to donate £500 (£20,000 in today's terms) to finance a new and much enlarged Rock Garden at Kew.

Starting with flat ground, it was laid out in 1882 between the west wall of the Herbaceous Ground and what was then the T-range of glasshouses (now replaced by the Princess of Wales Conservatory), taking the form of a

RIGHT: *Members of the ginger family are typically aromatic herbaceous plants inhabiting tropical forests;* Roscoea humeana, *however, is a diminutive relative from the Himalaya and the Lijiang Mountains in Yunnan, China, where it was found by the renowned plant hunters, George Forrest and Frank Kingdon Ward. The flowers, which appear before the leaves, can be seen in the Rock Garden growing beneath a* Cotoneaster microphyllum *var.* cochleatus, *from the Himalaya.*

Roscoea humeana
Rock Garden
7 June 1991

typical Pyrenean alpine valley, in which the water course dries up in summer. The soil, dug out to create a meandering main path simulating such a dry stream bed, was used to build the banks rising 4 metres (13 feet) high on either side and piled with rocks. As the path changed direction, so niches with different aspects could be made in the banks above. Beside the path occasional pools with cascading waterfalls provided suitable substrates for moisture-loving plants. When it was first laid out, one bay was filled with sea sand and planted with salt-loving plants native to Britain: for example, sea holly, *Eryngium maritimum* and sea pea, *Lathyrus japonicus*. This feature is, sadly, no longer there – although the rasping calls of black-headed gulls can be heard at Kew in winter.

Because funds were limited a hotchpotch of rocks was gleaned for the construction from any available source, including weathered Bath oolite and limestone from Cheddar cliffs, as well as marble and Portland oolite from a

RIGHT: *The short-stalked flowers of this member of the lily family nestle among the spreading leaf rosette. Native to south-east Spain, the plant frequents dry rocky places with limey soils.*

Androcymbium europeaum
Alpine House
14 January 1992

LEFT: *Although snowdrops are not brightly coloured, they are among the first bulbs to flower and are therefore an especially welcome sight on short winter days. From a distance, each nodding flower appears pure white, but on closer inspection it bears green patches. The first part of the generic name comes from the Greek word* gala *meaning milk.*

Snowdrop, Galanthus caucasicus
Alpine House
14 January 1992

RIGHT: *Wild ginger, so named from the gingery smell given off by the bruised rhizomes, is no relative of the true ginger but a member of the birthwort family. Pitcher-shaped flowers, opening out into three brownish calyx lobes to form a triangle, are produced from the base of the plant, well below the heart-shaped leaves.*

Wild ginger, Asarum speciosum
Alpine House
7 June 1991

ruin in Kew's Arboretum known as the 'Stone House'. Even so, there were not enough rocks to support the soil, so tree roots had to be used in places. Over the years the roots have rotted and have had to be replaced with rocks. When it was found that the original limestone both reflected too much light and failed to retain enough water, it was gradually replaced with Sussex sandstone, although the job was not completed until the 1960s.

New plants are continually being added to the Rock Garden; the current policy, however, is to grow only those collected from the wild or raised from wild seed – plants are not brought in from outside nurseries. When it was originally designed, the Rock Garden was planted haphazardly with neither systematic grouping into families nor geographical associations. Major re-landscaping, begun in 1991, extended the initial start made on grouping the plants within geographical regions, so that there is now an Asian area to the south and an Americas area around the central pond.

Among the American plants is an attractive evening primrose, *Oenothera missouriensis*, a native of dry, rocky limestone soils in the south central USA, which, like other evening primroses but not all oenotheras, is a night bloomer. New flowers open at night and last through much of the following day. Such plants typically bear white or pale yellow flowers and, when grown

LEFT: *It is, perhaps, surprising that cyclamens belong to the primrose family. The pot plants sold by florists are much larger than any wild species and have been derived from* Cyclamen persicum. C. trochopteanthum *grows on the Taurus Mountains in south-west Turkey up to the snow-line. Its attractive kidney-shaped leaves – dark green and silver above, carmine beneath – appear in autumn well before the carmine flowers.*

Cyclamen trochopteanthum
Alpine House
4 February 1991

LEFT: *Named after the ancient Greek physician Paeon, paeonies may be herbaceous or deciduous woody plants (tree paeonies). This herbaceous perennial, a native of the Balearic Islands and Corsica, has deep rose-pink single flowers set among leaves which have purple-red veins, stalks and undersides.*

Majorcan paeony, Paeonia cambessedesii
Alpine House
15 April 1991

RIGHT: Pleione formosana *is a deciduous orchid from East China and Taiwan, where it grows among mosses and rotting leaves on fallen logs and the base of tree trunks. The leaves and short-stalked, but large flowers are produced from an annual pseudobulb. These particularly attractive orchids can be grown in shallow pans indoors.*

Pleione formosana
Alpine House
15 April 1991

LEFT: *From January to April many different kinds of iris can be seen blooming in the Alpine House. Each iris flower usually has three large outer petals, known as 'falls', which hang down and three smaller 'standards'. This winter-flowering species from south and central Portugal and the Mediterranean region has orange lines on the 'falls'.*

Iris planifolia
Alpine House
10 January 1992

in private gardens, should preferably be positioned where they can be illuminated after dark by light from a window or driveway.

Seed collected from the wild on Kew expeditions has been used to propagate many of the perennials in the Rock Garden. There are also bulbs, while dwarf shrubs and conifers – notably several prostrate forms on top of the rock 'cliffs' – provide micro-habitats for shade-loving alpine plants.

Over the years, large bare rocks have become softened with living curtains of trailing plants, such as *Euphorbia myrsinites*, cascading over them. The sheer wealth of specimens (over 2,500 plants), many of which are tucked away in nooks and crannies, makes it easy to miss some on the first walk through the Rock Garden. Quite different plants will be seen by visitors retracing their steps and doubling back along the path. I find a pair of small binoculars useful for checking the identification labels or simply for appreciating the beauty of individual flowers high up on the rocky outcrops. Spring is the time to enjoy the Rock Garden at its best; however, throughout the spring and summer, weekly visits are like a voyage of discovery as plants previously passed by catch the eye when they burst into bloom.

In the early days, although the range of plants was not nearly so extensive as it is today, the Rock Garden none the less attracted a great deal of interest. Yet field botanists were only too well aware that the relatively mild Thames Valley winters, with irregular periods of freezing alternating with mild spells, in no way simulated natural conditions where plants were normally covered by a protective blanket of snow for six months of the year. During the milder winter spells at Kew, alpines would begin to grow, only to be pruned back by frost, drying wind or persistent rain.

In 1887, therefore, five years after the Rock Garden was made, the first Alpine House was constructed; it was enlarged in 1891 and again in 1936. But no attempt was made to landscape the plants, which were simply displayed in regimented rows on a raised bench to either side of a central gangway.

In 1981 a futuristic Alpine House with a pyramidal roof was opened in the old Melon Yard to the north of the Jodrell Laboratory. This was designed in such a way as to allow the maximum light transmission, yet have variable ventilation. Three flights of electronically controlled ventilators on each of the four faces of the pyramid open automatically as temperatures rise, closing in a high wind and dropping below horizontal when rain falls. Rainwater runs off the roof into a surrounding moat and then into an underground tank which is used for watering the plants. Gone are the benches with rows and rows of pots, so typical of early alpine houses. Instead both the banks around the moat and much of the interior have been landscaped as a rock garden with Sussex sandstone, planted with almost 3,000 different montane subjects on permanent display. Plants from the southern hemisphere and the Balearic Islands, as well as from equatorial mountain regions, can be seen inside the Alpine House. Additional colour and interest are provided by potted plants and bulbs, either plunged into the front of the beds or displayed on benches hiding the controls. These plants are replaced frequently from the nursery stock so that there are always some flowers on display, although May is the peak month for seeing the largest array of alpine blooms.

A peat gulley runs through the western side of the Alpine House, dividing an acidic scree area near the south entrance from an alkaline area for lime-loving plants. There is also an alkaline scree on the east side of the south entrance. In the third landscaped area is a small pool fed by a waterfall. The

BELOW: Leucocoryne *is a genus of lily relatives from Chile. When several bulbs are planted together, their multi-flowered umbels produce a wonderful flora display in a cool conservatory.*

Glory of the sun, Leucocoryne sp.
Alpine House
20 May 1991

LEFT: *Powerful sodium lamps extend the short days of a British winter for equatorial montane plants growing in the refrigerated bench within the Alpine House. In the foreground can be seen the white-felted leaved espeletias and puyas from South America, with a yellow flowering spike of* Espeletia schultzii *from Venezuela behind.*

Equatorial montane bench lit with sodium lamps in winter
Alpine House
28 November 1991

RIGHT: Lachenalias *are bulbous plants from South Africa, where they are known as Cape-cowslips – a rather misleading name, since they are not remotely like cowslips. The tubular or bell-shaped flowers may be pendulous, horizontal or upright and are arranged on a spike.*
L. *'tricolor' has multi-coloured spikes, red at the top with the yellow, pendulous flowers shading to green flared tips.*

Lachenalia *'tricolor'*
Alpine House
1 April 1990

pool contains some aquatics, while bogland plants grow in the surrounding peaty margins, including male plants of the diminutive *Gunnera hamiltonii* from Stewart Island off the southern tip of New Zealand's South Island.

The problems montane plants have to face are similar to those encountered by desert flora, namely ways and means of conserving water, for at high altitude (or high latitude in the case of arctic-alpines) water uptake is impossible when the ground is frozen. The majority of these plants are small, compact perennials which grow very slowly. Cushion formers are not uncommon and small, inrolled leaves help to conserve water. A thick cuticle or a hairy coating are both adaptations to reduce water loss by evaporation through the leaf surface. Careful observation of plants grown in the Alpine House will reveal examples of all such adaptations.

The graceful, pendulous-flowered snowbell, *Soldanella alpina*, has an ingenious way of combating the cold. By fermenting sugars it releases heat and melts the snow all around it. The glacier buttercup, *Ranunculus glacialis*, concentrates the sap inside its cells which serves the same function as 'anti-freeze' by lowering the freezing point of the cell sap.

Anyone who is familiar with the montane floras of Europe, North America or Asia will know that many of the flowers are brightly coloured. It is, therefore, something of a surprise and a disappointment to discover that the New Zealand alpine is very limited in its colour range. The majority of flowers – even gentians and forget-me-nots, *Myosotis* spp. – are white and have short corolla tubes. The probable explanation is the paucity of native insects with long tongues, such as bees and butterflies, which are attracted

by bright colours. Instead the flowers are pollinated by a range of short-tongued insects that are lured by scent rather than by colour. This lack of colour among the flowers is, however, more than compensated for by the brightly coloured, fleshy fruits, such as those produced by coprosmas, gaultherias, pratias and pernettyias.

In the centre of the Alpine House is a cooled bench for growing tropical montane and arctic-alpine species. Refrigerated coils, covered by 30 centimetres (1 foot) of sand, maintain low ground temperatures for specialist montane plants, including several from the African equatorial mountains, Mount Kenya and Mount Elgon, where daylight and darkness are of equal length and frosts occur each night. The potted plants are plunged into the sand which drops to 5°C (41°F) at night and rises to 21°C (69.8°F) by day. The short British winter days are extended with high-pressure sodium lamps positioned directly above the bench to provide a twelve-hour day – essential for growth to take place.

A feature common to both the Andean and African equatorial mountains is the occurrence of gigantic forms of genera which have much smaller relatives at lower altitudes. For example, on Mounts Kenya (5,199 metres/17,057 feet in Kenya), Elgon (4,321 metres/14,176 feet on the Kenyan/Ugandan border) and Ruwenzori (5,109 metres/16,761 feet in Uganda) gigantic tree-like senecios up to 9 metres (30 feet) high and lobelias up to 8 metres (26 feet) high – specific to each mountain – occur. None of these could seem further removed from the invasive annual weed of gardens, *Senecio vulgaris* (better known as groundsel) or the small, blue-flowered lobelias used for summer bedding. As new leaves open at the top of the afro-alpine giants, so old ones wither and hang down at the base, absorbing heat by day and helping to insulate the stem at night.

All these gigantic herbs initially develop huge, cabbage-like leaf rosettes which grow for many years before a flower spike is produced. The inner leaves of the rosettes close up at night to protect the central growing point. Field work done on Mount Kenya has led to the discovery that lobelia rosettes close up less tightly on cloudy than on clear nights when the temperature drops much lower. The temperature in a tight night bud remains above 2°C (35.6°F) even when outside temperatures fall to −5°C (23°F). The lobelias cradle a small pool of water in the centre of their rosettes in which secretions from the leaf bases produce a viscous liquid – another case of a self-generated 'anti-freeze'. In the Andes it is the espeletias and puyas that grow to a huge size, notably the bromeliad *Puya raimondii*, which produces a flowering spike up to 6 metres (20 feet) high and then dies. Senecios and espeletias both belong to the daisy family and the giant forms have thick felt on their leaves which helps to insulate the bud at night.

A small part of the refrigerated bench in the Alpine House contains Arctic plants, including the yellow-flowered Arctic poppy, *Papaver radicatum*, and primulas. During the winter they are moved into a cold store and kept in the dark at −6°C (21.2°F) in conditions similiar to those they would experience beneath a snowdrift. When the plants are replaced in the refrigerated bench for the summer, their daylight hours are increased by the use of overhead lamps (including long wavelengths of infra-red light) to simulate the long, Arctic summer days.

Outside the east entrance of the Alpine House are several sinks and troughs, landscaped on a miniature scale. Some contain tufa (a lightweight and porous limestone rock) in which alpines are planted directly into natural crevices or into man-made holes. Near the south entrance to the house is a raised bed surrounded by lawn, also landscaped with tufa rocks, while in beds on the shady north side of the Jodrell Laboratory a peat garden has been made for displaying Japanese montane and woodland plants.

Adjacent to the Rock Garden, beside the path running along the east side of the Princess of Wales Conservatory, scree beds elevated above the level of the surrounding soil allow water to drain away quickly. These special conditions have made it possible to extend the range of montane plants that can now be grown outside at Kew.

Few people who visit the Gardens will be aware of a new rock garden within the central courtyard of the Herbarium and Library. Constructed of rocks and gravel on the roof of a large, new extension, it contains not a single plant, for it is a Japanese stone garden designed by the architect of the building, Peter Riddington, and completed in 1989. In the style of a Zen Buddhist garden, the gravel is combed into a ridged pattern with a wide-pronged wooden rake, while two pavilions, structurally essential to allow smoke expulsion from the building below in the event of fire, add both height and colour. This is a very different oriental concept from that of the Pagoda and other Chinese-style buildings constructed over two centuries ago in the time of Sir William Chambers, but where better to contemplate the future of Kew than in a garden designed for meditation?

High-altitude montane plants, growing well above the tree line, are not under such intense pressure from man's activities as are those of more accessible habitats. But at lower altitudes mountain forests are being lost both to

ABOVE: *The blade of each petal is completely lacking in this columbine, so that the cluster of stamens protrudes well below the five brick red spurs tipped in yellow. The natural home of this aquilegia is in wet areas where there is seepage on to serpentine rocks in the Coast Ranges of California.*

Columbine, Aquilegia exima
Raised bed outside Alpine House
4 August 1991

logging and to agriculture. Such forests act as huge natural sponges, absorbing rain and snow-melt water and gradually releasing it over a period of many days. Therefore, when heavy monsoon rain falls on ground which has been completely cleared of trees, as has happened in parts of the Himalaya, the water cannot be stored: instead, torrents of water gouge out soil and carry it down to the lowland plains, causing not only severe flooding but also untold damage and loss of life. Furthermore, huge silt loads are discharged into the sea, affecting the marine environment as well as commercial fisheries. Here, then, is an example of how damage to one habitat can have knock-on effects in another location far removed from it. Sadly it is all too easy for visitors, while enjoying the delights of the Alpine House and Rock Garden at Kew, to distance themselves from such major environmental problems on the other side of the world.

RIGHT: *All* Meconopsis, *with the exception of* M. cambrica *from western Europe, come from the Himalaya or the mountains of western China. Blue Himalayan poppies are the best known, but yellow-, white- and even red-flowered species also occur. Typical of the genus, the petals are so tightly folded inside the bud that when they unfurl they resemble crushed tissue paper. This striking species comes from western China and Tibet and is grown in a bed outside the Alpine House.*

Meconopsis punicea
Outside Alpine House
22 May 1991

CHAPTER SEVEN

GRASSLAND PLANTS

*Just three species of grassland plants —
rice, wheat and maize — provide more than
half the food consumed by man;
grasslands are also home to some orchids,
among the most beautiful plants on
earth. Other grasses grown at Kew include
both temperate and tropical bamboos.*

IN PARTS OF the world with low rainfall, trees do not form forests with closed canopies; instead they thin out into wooded grasslands. In temperate regions these are transitional areas between forests and deserts, situated in the heart of continents. Wherever it lies, grassland terrain, which is typically flat or rolling, is subjected to alternating hot and cold seasons. The most extensive natural grasslands are the steppes of central Asia, the prairies of North America, the veldt of South Africa and the pampas of Argentina. These areas provide food for seed-eating rodents as well as for large herbivores which, in turn, attract predators and scavengers. The constant cropping of grass by herbivores coupled with spasmodic fires help to maintain the grassland and prevent trees from developing and casting shadows which inhibit the growth of grasses.

Natural grasslands the world over are much more than simply a collection of grasses. After the rains come in east Africa, the flowers of bulbs and other plants enliven the savanna with bold splashes of colour. Bulbs from grassland areas in Europe and South Africa can be seen flowering at Kew on the Bulb Patio in the Duke's Garden.

On the wetter east side of the vast North American prairies, the grass is longer than on the short-grass prairie to the west. Before these natural grasslands began to be lost to the plough, they supported huge bison herds

LEFT: *A lone Thomson's gazelle seeks shade under a solitary tree on the rolling grassland plains within the Masai Mara Reserve in Kenya. In August, after several months without rain, the savannah grasses turn a rich golden colour, punctuated only by strips of green vegetation bordering the water courses.*

estimated to total some sixty million in 1800. Until that time Indians took only a few animals for their food and clothing. Then white man moved in and the slaughter began; within forty years the herds were down to five and a half million, and by 1900 fewer than 300 wild animals remained on the North American continent. As more and more prairies were given over to crops, so the natural permanent grassland cover was lost, and when this ground lay barren there was no protection for the bare, dry topsoil. Huge areas were lost as high winds whipped up severe dust storms – notably in the 1930s – creating one vast dust bowl across five states. The solution to this man-made problem was to create windbreaks: from 1935 to 1942 more than 222 million trees were planted in a 320-kilometre- (200-mile)-wide band stretching for a distance of some 1,610 kilometres (1,000 miles).

Wildebeest, although much smaller than bison, are none the less impressive when seen migrating *en masse* across the Serengeti Plains in Tanzania or further north in Kenya's Masai Mara. These tropical east African grasslands are subject to distinct wet and dry seasons. Here, after many months of drought, the land becomes a sea of golden grass as the stems and leaves above ground die back; but once the rains begin the grasses spring to life and the land is green again. The wildebeest prefer to graze the short grass and move on when it becomes too long.

Grasses are able not only to tolerate long periods of drought, but also to survive burning. Their fibrous roots arising from a deep system of rhizomes can extract water very efficiently from the soil when rain falls. As every gardener knows, nipping out the leading shoot of a dicotyledonous herbaceous plant encourages the side shoots to sprout, thereby producing a bushier specimen. This is not the case with monocotyledonous plants such as grasses for, when a lawn is cut, tillers form from the nodes and the grass continues to grow from the base of the leaves. Even when grasses are burnt, new leaves will sprout up from the rhizomes which are untouched by fire.

Indeed, one of the ways in which man manages grasslands is to burn areas in rotation. Burning not only removes the long, dry grass, but also stimulates new growth by the release of mineral salts back on to the land.

With the exception of highly ornamental types, most grasses are rarely spared a second glance; yet we could not live without them, for as well as natural grasslands there are man-made meadows that are cut for hay, pastures which provide grazing land for stock, and cornfields and rice paddies that produce essential grain to feed the world. All our staple crops – wheat, oats, barley, rye, maize, sorghum, millet, rice and sugar cane, as well as bamboo – are members of the grass family. Grain-producing grasses are referred to as cereals, a term derived from the name of Ceres, the Greek goddess of grain.

Most of the grasses grown at Kew are grouped together in the Grass Garden (beside the Aquatic Garden) which contains some 600 different species, ornamental as well as economic, from the five continents. The beds look most striking in autumn when clumps of the pampas grass, *Cortaderia selloana*, produce their magnificent white plumes. Two central beds are planted with cereals, one containing temperate and the other sub-tropical examples. In temperate regions the major cereal crop is wheat, and the modern varieties of bread wheat, *Triticum aestivum*, have been bred to produce higher yields and resist disease more effectively than their ancestors. Here comparisons can be made between modern and primitive wheat cultivars. Bread wheat produces grain that is ground into flour not only for bread, but also for cakes, biscuits and pastry; the flour from durum wheat, *T. durum*, is

BELOW: *A detail of the large feathery panicle of the North American switch grass shows the orange pollen-producing stamens and the white feathery stigmas. Gardeners will be familiar with the cultivar* Panicum virgatum *'rubrum' which has leaves that turn reddish-brown late in summer.*

Switch grass, Panicum virgatum
Grass Garden
10 June 1992

used for making pasta. The small-seeded, long-awned einkorn, *T. monococcum*, was probably one of the ancestors of our modern wheats.

Sub-tropical cereals grown at Kew include maize, *Zea mays,* and several kinds of millet and sorghum. The male and female flowers (or inflorescences) of maize are quite distinct and equally conspicuous. Male flowers with pollen-covered anthers are produced at the upper end of the stem, while the female ones develop lower down with long tassels emerging from the top of the cob. After pollination the cob fattens as it ripens. Maize is the only cereal crop to have originated in the USA, where it is known simply as corn; in Central and South America it is called mealies.

Other beds in the Grass Garden display ornamental grasses, some producing unusual variegated leaves or particularly striking flower spikes. A variety of grasses suitable for lawn turf is grown in brick-edged beds and, because they are kept mown, these do not flower. Other grasses, however, produce some very attractive flower spikes. As the flowers are pollinated by wind, they lack attractants for insect or animal pollinators, such as colourful petals or nectar, but what they lack in colour, individual grass flowers more than make

BELOW: *The Grass Garden looks its best in summer and early autumn, when clumps of pampas grass produce their huge creamy flower spikes.*

Pampas grass, Cortaderia selloana *var.* pumila
Grass Garden
1 October 1991

ABOVE: *After wheat and rice, maize or Indian corn is the most important grain crop. The female flowers end in tassels that hang down. Ornamental varieties, which produce cobs with brightly coloured or variegated fruits, are popular in the United States.*

Female flower of maize, Zea 'Silvermine'
Grass Garden
25 August 1991

LEFT: *Once the grains begin to ripen in the Grass Garden, a flock of sparrows can invariably be seen foraging. If disturbed from one clump, they will lift off and move on to another. In years when some of the cereals are enclosed in a mesh cage, the choice of grain becomes more limited for these opportunist feeders.*

Sparrow
Grass Garden
25 August 1991

up for in exquisite shape and form – not readily apparent to the human eye without the aid of a hand lens. The flowering spike contains many spikelets, each of which may consist of one, two or many florets. The spikelets may be arranged in a loose panicle (as in oats and rice), a dense panicle (as in millet), or a spike (as in wheat).

A feature shared by all wind-pollinated flowers is the production of copious microscopic pollen grains which are wafted in the gentlest of breezes from one flower to another. Grass pollen so dispersed is the prime cause of hay fever in both Europe, the USA and Australia, as many sufferers know to their cost. The pollen count, broadcast daily, is produced by aerobiologists analysing the amount of pollen in the air during the previous twenty-four hours and taking into account the immediate forecast. It represents the average number of grass pollen grains per cubic metre of air caught in a special trap during a

RIGHT: *Man y garden varieties have arisen from* Miscar thus sinensis, *a grass native to Japan and China. This variegated one, known as zebra grass, has horizontal yellowish-white bands on the leaves. Reminiscent of feather dusters, coppery-red flowering panicles, broadest at the top, appear in autumn and will persist through the winter.*

Zebra grass, Miscanthus sinensis *'Zebrinus'*
Grass Garden
25 August 1991

twenty-four-hour period. Since the microscopic structure of pollen grains is unique to each family of plants, the origin of the pollen can be pinpointed every day. Most people who are allergic to pollen begin to suffer when the pollen count reaches 50 grains per cubic metre of air, and counts can rise to 200 in June and July. Rain washes the pollen out of the air, so a wet summer is good news for hay fever sufferers.

Among several tropical grasses grown in Kew's Palm House, two are of great economic importance. One of these, rice, *Oryza sativa*, is the staple food of more than half the world's population. It has been grown in India and China for at least four millennia and the Indians introduced wet rice cultivation to south-east Asia almost 2,000 years ago. The grains are grown in flooded paddy fields and the seedlings then planted out by hand. When ripe, the rice stems are cut and hand-threshed. Rice is primarily a tropical crop,

although it will grow in the sub-tropics and can therefore be cultivated anywhere from 45° north to 40° south of the Equator. Highly labour-intensive methods are simply not economic for rice-growing areas within Europe, such as the Camargue in France, where the latest laser technology is used to check the level of the rice fields before flooding. In addition the French fields are drained before harvesting to enable combine harvesters to be used for extracting rice grains in a similar way to wheat.

Sugar cane, *Saccharum officinarum*, is a tropical grass with a distinctively jointed stem and, when grown commercially, is cut before the attractive, white, feathery panicles appear. While all green plants produce sugars, only a few do so in large enough quantities to make their extraction worthwhile on a commercial scale. Nearly all the world's sugar originates from two plants,

RIGHT: *Einkorn is one of several kinds of wheat grown in the Grass Garden as a demonstration of the history of wheat. Also known as small spelt, einkorn produces small, bearded ears. Unlike modern wheat cultivars, the grains cannot easily be threshed.*

Einkorn, Triticum monococcum
Grass Garden
4 August 1991

LEFT: *Stipas are spear grasses which originate from Spain and North America. Esparto grass, Stipa tenacissima, is cultivated for its strong fibres used for making paper, mats and ropes. Perennial cortaderias form such massive clumps, they are ideal as specimen plants.*

Stipa gigantea *and* Cortaderia richardii
Grass Garden
2 August 1991

LEFT: *A native of North America, Europe and Asia, fox-tail barley can become a troublesome weed, but the dried flower spikes make attractive additions to any display of everlasting plants. The arching feathery flower spikes are somewhat reminiscent of a squirrel's tail, hence the alternative name of squirrel-tail grass.*

Fox-tail barley, Hordeum jubatum
Grass Garden
29 June 1989

RIGHT: Pennisetum *grasses originate from both warm temperate zones and the tropics. Feathertop is a perennial from Ethiopia which is grown as an annual in Britain. Each flowering spike bears long white awns and resembles a bottle brush.*

Feathertop, Pennisetum villosum
Grass Garden
29 June 1989

sugar cane and sugar beet, *Beta vulgaris*. The sticky brown liquid separated from the sugar crystals after sugar cane is crushed is known as molasses. This is sold as black treacle or used in the manufacture of yeasts for baking and brewing. Crushed sugar canes, known as bagasse, are used in paper and plastic manufacture and as food for cattle.

Two grass plants, sugar cane and maize, are now being utilized to produce bioalcohol. This liquid energy, which is more convenient to store than biogas (see p.15), is beginning to replace fossil hydrocarbons in some countries and has the added advantage of being renewable. Large-scale projects are producing ethyl alcohol from sugars and starches in the USA and Brazil. Already almost a third of the latter country's energy is derived from biofuel, produced by the fermentation of sugar, which is used to power more than three million specially adapted cars. To prevent this alcohol from being drunk, 3 per cent petrol has to be added. In addition, some eight million cars are run on a 78/22 petrol/alcohol mixture.

Bamboos, a distinct group of grasses with woody stems or culms, occur in temperate and tropical regions of Asia as well as Central and South America. They are essentially plants which prefer moist and shady conditions within forests or forest margins; although they can themselves form forests. Bamboos provide food for a variety of animals, none more famous than China's giant panda. Loss of habitat in China's Sichuan and Gansu provinces, as well as hunting by man, have contributed to the panda's decline, exacerbated by the tendency of all the bamboo food plants in an area to synchronize their flowering and then die. Encroachment into natural forests by agriculture has fragmented bamboo stands into isolated pockets, which means that when the

LEFT: Melica macra *is an Argentinean grass which is equally attractive when a mass of flowering spikes arise from a clump or when individual spikes are used in dried flower arrangements. The generic name is derived from the Greek* meli, *meaning honey.*

Melica macra
Grass Garden
13 June 1992

BELOW: *Raindrops provide an ephemeral silvery contrast to this bamboo from China.*

Bamboo, Thamnocalamus dracocephalus
Bamboo Garden
26 October 1991

bamboo in one area flowers and dies – as happened in 1975 – many giant pandas literally starve to death before they can reach another source.

Within the Far East in particular, bamboos have many uses: the considerable strength of long, tough-stemmed and wide-diameter types recommends them for construction purposes, while leaves may be plaited or woven and new shoots eaten. In China there can be few objects that have not at one time been made from bamboo – roofs, baskets, paper, mats, fencing, tree guards, fishing rods, walking sticks, push-chairs, flutes, rafts, yokes, coat hangers, ladders, cantilevered devices and scaffolding, to name but a few. There is a written account, dating from AD 347, of bamboo tubes being used as pipelines – passing beneath roads or above them on trestles – to carry natural gas many kilometres overland.

Hardy bamboos from the temperate parts of Asia and South America can be grown out of doors in Britain, although a few may need protection in a cold winter. Several types are grown in the Grass Garden, some in the Palm House and the Temperate House at Kew, but most of the collection is in the Bamboo Garden, made during the winter of 1891–2 in a disused gravel pit east of the Rhododendron Dell. The sunken site offers some measure of protection during severe weather.

Among the bamboos grown in the Temperate House is *Arundinaria simonii*. The heavenly bamboo, *Nandina domestica*, a native of China which produces attractive, red fruits that persist all winter, is not a true bamboo at all. It is now grown outside up against the wall of the House.

BELOW: *The golden colour of this variegated bamboo from Japan develops to the full only when the plant is grown in a sunny position. Indeed, in a shady situation the leaves gradually turn green. New canes are also more likely to produce good colour.*

Arundinaria auricoma
Outside the Princess of Wales Conservatory
7 June 1991

Some bamboos can spread very rapidly, running in all directions by means of underground rhizomes, so that one species can easily become completely entangled with another. Kew's first attempt at containing vigorous species in the Bamboo Garden involved surrounding each clump with old conveyor belting; although flexible, it began to break up and a substitute had to be found. Black polypropylene sheeting is now used, driven vertically into the ground to a depth of about 1 metre (3 feet).

Bamboos range in size from short plants suitable for use as ground cover to giant trees. Some of the tropical kinds grow exceedingly quickly, as much as 1–2 metres (3–6½ feet) per day. The giant bamboo, *Gigantochloa verticillata*, which grows in the central transept of the Palm House, will reach up to 25 metres (82 feet) in Asia, so it has to have its stems cut repeatedly to prevent it from reaching the glass dome. All bamboos have jointed, hollow culms and most are evergreen. Colour variations among ornamental bamboos include black or purple culms; yellow culms streaked with green; and golden and variegated leaves.

A phenomenon known as guttation, found among grasses (including bamboos) but not unique to them, occurs on warm, humid nights when the water pressure builds up in the roots, causing drops to be exuded near the leaf tips. The large size of the drops and their precise position makes it easy to distinguish guttation from dew, which takes the form of a random scattering of water drops all over the leaves. The end product of guttation can be seen early in the morning.

All British grasslands are man-made; they developed after forests were cleared, initially for arable purposes and later to create pasture for grazing stock, chiefly sheep. At much the same time as the sheep populations declined, rabbits began to increase in numbers. Thus one herbivore took over from another, maintaining the short turf so essential for smaller and rarer chalk grassland flowers – notably wild orchids – to survive. If scrub is not kept in check by grazing stock or rabbits, it will invade grassland and a succession of larger plants will develop until ultimately a forest returns.

After the disease myxomatosis reached Britain in 1953, the rabbit population plummeted. The immediate effect was a spectacular flowering of the grasslands, with some rare plants blooming for the first time in many years. However, when the grazing pressure was removed, vigorous plants and scrub began to invade chalk grasslands, choking short plants, including wild orchids. Concern was so great that the then Nature Conservancy Council (the NCC, now English Nature) used a flock of peripatetic sheep which grazed on successive chalk grassland reserves in southern Britain.

Habitat destruction and change of land use in Europe have resulted in the decline of all wild orchids during the last three decades. Almost a quarter of Britain's native species are endangered. Ten of these are listed in the Wildlife and Countryside Act 1981 (with the 1987 amendments), which makes it illegal to remove any plant from the wild without a permit from English Nature or from the appropriate bodies in Wales and Scotland.

The dust-like seeds of orchids are among the smallest produced by any flowering plants. They are so tiny that they contain virtually no food supplies of their own. Moreover it has been known for almost a century that an orchid seed will survive and grow in the wild only if it lands beside a certain kind of fungus with which it forms a mutually beneficial symbiotic association. The fungus enters the orchid embryo, feeding it during the initial weeks until a shoot appears. Later the fungus (which may associate with just a single orchid

RIGHT: *The giant bamboo thrives in the Palm House where it reaches the greatest height of all the grasses grown at Kew. The young shoots are edible, while the tough canes are used for rafters and posts inside Asian houses. A section of the cane, between one node and the next, makes a convenient water carrier.*

Giant bamboo, Gigantochloa verticillata
Palm House
5 September 1991

LEFT: *Following a warm, humid night, obvious water drops can often be seen hanging from the tips of grass leaves early the next morning. These are not dew drops, for they have been exuded from pores in the grass leaves.*

Grasses showing guttation
Arboretum
17 May 1991

species) forms a symbiotic assocation with the orchid root. This association is known as a mychorrhiza.

For over half a century tropical orchids and countless cultivars have been propagated successfully in the laboratory, but temperate terrestrial kinds have been more problematic. As time was clearly running out for some of the rarest European wild orchids, there arose a pressing need to develop successful propagation techniques for them. Therefore a research programme – known as the Sainsbury Orchid Conservation Project – to raise British and European orchids in bulk from seed was initiated at Kew in 1983. Fungi isolated from the roots of adult orchids were used to infect seeds to increase the germination rate. It was found necessary to keep the culture in the dark in the early stages of germination and some species had to be chilled. After several species raised from seed had flowered in glasshouses, the next step was to see if orchid seedlings would survive to flower out of doors. During the autumn of 1987 seedlings of the Jersey orchid, *Orchis laxiflora*, were planted out at Wakehurst Place; in the following May seven plants flowered and a year later many more flowering spikes were produced. Plantings of other orchids were made at Kew in an area not open to the public. Here several green-winged orchids, *Orchis morio*, and spotted orchids, *Dactylorhiza fuchsii*, flowered, as well as a lone bee orchid, *Ophrys apifera*.

After these successes efforts were concentrated on raising the rarest British wild orchids. At one time there were more people involved with the re-introduction of lady's slipper orchid, *Cypripedium calceolus*, to the wild than there were seedlings! Each successive year sees an expansion in knowledge of the cultivation of British and European terrestrial orchids and a greater

RIGHT: *Drainage and cultivation of old damp pastures in southern England have reduced the habitat favoured by the green-winged orchid. Recognized by the green lines on the two lateral sepals, it is one of several British native grassland species introduced to the Conservation Area at Kew. Using micropropagation techniques, Kew scientists have been able to propagate several rarer British orchids by sowing their minute seeds with the relevant symbiotic fungus essential for germination to take place.*

Green-winged orchid, Orchis morio
Conservation Area
17 May 1991

appreciation of the pitfalls. For example, it is now realized that some of the mycorrhizal fungi, when kept in culture for considerable time, lose their effectiveness in promoting the germination of orchid seeds. Currently work is being done to rear other extremely rare British wild orchids, including red helleborine, *Cephalanthera rubra*; lizard orchid, *Himantoglossum hircinum*; spider orchid, *Ophrys sphegodes*; military orchid, *Orchis militaris*; and monkey orchid, *Orchis simia*.

Perhaps the most undervalued of all plants, grasses provide more than half the food consumed by man from just three kinds – rice, wheat and maize; they also help to stabilize soils and can even be used as a source of renewable fuel. Ornamental grasses, the beauty of which is very much under-rated, deserve to be planted more widely and appreciated to a far greater extent.

CHAPTER EIGHT

WILDLIFE

*Any large parkland or garden is
bound to attract wildlife, and Kew is no
exception. Forty-five species of birds
are known to nest in the Gardens, from the
common sparrow to the great crested
grebe; butterflies and insects abound; and
resident mammals include moles,
voles, hedgehogs and grey squirrels. Kew also
has its own flocks of ornamental
wildfowl which are, in themselves, a major
attraction for visitors.*

EXTENSIVE parks and gardens which have a variety of habitats including water as well as expansive lawns, scrubland and woodlands – not to mention a galaxy of flowers and fruits – naturally attract wildlife. Kew Gardens is no exception; indeed it is a veritable haven for wildlife residents and visitors. However, while many people delight in seeing wildlife, it should not be forgotten that the gardeners strive to keep a balance between controlling pests and encouraging wildlife that will not damage or destroy any part of the living Plant Collection.

Since people visit the Gardens throughout the year, much of the wildlife is remarkably tame and will tolerate a fairly close approach – a great boon to the keen photographer. The best place to see a variety of wildlife – notably wild birds, but also rabbits and squirrels – is the Queen's Cottage Grounds. These 16 hectares (40 acres) of woodland were given to the nation by Queen Victoria in 1898 to commemorate her Diamond Jubilee. At the time she made the following request: 'The Queen earnestly trusts that this unique spot may be preserved in its present beautiful and natural condition.' Since

LEFT: *A flock of Canada geese,* Branta canadensis,
*graze a lawn adjacent to the Palm House in November.
They tend to frequent the paved area around the Pond
throughout the year, but much larger flocks congregate
to feed on the grassy areas beside the Lake early
on a winter's morning.*

LEFT: *After coot chicks hatch, the female broods them while the male forages for water plants which are brought back to the nest. After three to four days, both parents leave the nest and, with much squawking, the bravest chick gingerly scrambles to the nest rim, totters and plops into the water. The others soon follow and they swim off to join their parents who both work hard, submerging for food, then suddenly bouncing back up to the surface again.*

Coot chicks, Fulica atra
The Lake
28 April 1991

RIGHT: *Great crested grebes move back and forth from inland waters to the coast but, unlike black-headed gulls, they nest at Kew – either on the Pond or on the Lake – and move elsewhere in winter. The nest, often floating on water, is made of damp reeds. The grebes feed by diving beneath the surface for fish, tadpoles and newts, as well as plants.*

Great crested grebe, Podiceps cristatus
The Pond
13 June 1989

LEFT: *Early morning or late evening are the most likely times to see a heron at Kew, either on the Lake or the Pond. During the rest of the day, they fly north-west to islands in the Thames or across the other side of the river to perch in willows.*

Grey heron, Ardea cinerea
The Lake
28 October 1991

then it has been maintained as a magical wild part to the Gardens with access only along fenced paths.

In May, as the beech trees unfurl their fresh green leaves, the area is transformed by spectacular azure carpets of bluebells – a colour combination which for me epitomizes spring in southern Britain. Encroaching into some parts of the blue swards are drifts of taller, acid-yellow perfoliate alexanders, a much daintier version of the more vigorous and better known alexanders of coastal haunts. The accidental combination of colours is most striking and is one of which the artist-turned-garden designer, Gertrude Jekyll, would have approved. Indeed, she recommended planting a single yellow flower among a drift of blue so that the complementary colour would further enhance the blueness.

The most conspicuous wildlife is, without doubt, the birds. Each year, more than eighty different species of wild birds are recorded as visitors to the Kew grounds or in the immediate vicinity outside. From Riverside Avenue, a walk running parallel to the Thames, grey herons regularly perch in willows bordering Syon Reach and, come the evening (or early morning), some fly into the Gardens where they can often be seen stalking along the margins of the Lake or the Pond. Since the Sir Joseph Banks Building was completed in 1990, herons have taken to roosting overnight on the wooden bridge spanning the lakes adjacent to it.

As many as forty-five species of wild birds nest in the Gardens, some in quite bizarre places: robins have nested in the Princess of Wales Conservatory, kestrels in the chimney of the Palm House and, in 1991, a pair of coots repeatedly attempted to nest on top of the fountain jet in the Banks Pond, only to have their efforts thwarted each time the fountain was turned on. The fact that we can see great crested grebes regularly nesting on the Pond or the Lake is fortunate indeed, for these attractive water birds were almost wiped out in Britain during the last century when their feathers were much sought after by the millinery trade. By 1860 only forty-two pairs of great crested grebes remained in Britain, but the man-made aquatic habitats – including flooded gravel pits – in southern Britain provided suitable nesting

sites which led to their gradual recovery. Long before nest-building commences, look out for the grebe's distinctive and elaborate courtship displays which include diving and emerging in a penguin-like stance, head-shaking and, perhaps the most famous of all, the weed-presentation dance culminating in the pair rising out of the water towards each other carrying water weed streaming from their bills.

Coots and moorhens choose old tree stumps, reed clumps or any structure on which they can build their nests above the water level. Their fluffy chicks take to the water within a few days of hatching, looking not unlike over-sized bumblebees as they dart over the surface. Even after the chicks leave the nest, their parents work hard, submerging to forage on aquatic plants to feed their offspring before they learn to dive themselves. After expending so much effort, it is unfortunate that many chicks fall prey to carrion crows. Moorhens, with their conspicuous red head shield and red bill tipped with yellow, can often be seen grazing on the lawns early in the morning. When disturbed a moorhen walks away, intermittently displaying the white flashes beneath the tail in a decidedly jerky fashion. If you are lucky, you may find a kingfisher perching on a label in the waterlily pond within the Aquatic Garden. Here, too, mallard and moorhens swim around, playing 'dodgems' among the forest of labels.

Robins are remarkably tame and during the winter whenever a visitor stops to read a label or photograph a plant, one will invariably alight on the ground near by. When no food is forthcoming, however, it will soon flit off elsewhere. Blackbirds can be seen foraging for food and nesting materials in the leaf litter laid as a mulch on beds. Like robins, blackbirds are highly territorial and can often be seen atop one of the brick pillars bordering the wall of the Herbaceous Ground, calling loudly to proclaim their territory.

A bird which no one – birdwatcher or not – can miss is the Canada goose, for in winter it is by far the most vociferous and numerous of the wild birds, moving around in large flocks grazing on the lawns. Very effective peripatetic lawnmowers they may be, but their prodigious droppings tend to detract from their usefulness. These black-headed, white-chinned geese

were introduced to ornamental collections in Britain from North America almost three centuries ago (indeed, it was fashionable to have these birds in the grounds of stately homes around the time of the reign of Charles II), but it took a long time to establish itself in the wild. When the first national Canada goose census was organized by the British Trust for Ornithology (BTO) in 1953, some 2,600–3,600 birds were counted in Britain. Since this date, the Canada goose population has grown rapidly, increasing almost threefold (10,000–10,500 birds) by the time of the 1967–9 Wildfowl Trust survey. By 1988 their numbers had reached 51,000 and the Wildfowl and Wetlands Trust (WWT) estimate that they are increasing at a rate of $8\frac{1}{2}$ per cent per annum. The sharpest population rise is occurring in the Thames Basin where it is estimated that there are now some 25,000 birds, and there could be as many as 80,000 by the year 2000 if they continue to increase at the same rate. The rapid population increase in the 1950s seems to be linked with the geese taking to breeding in gravel pits and also utilizing – much to farmers' chagrin – winter wheat as a winter feed. In the spring and summer, Kew has thirty pairs of nesting Canada geese and 110 non-breeding birds; but come the winter, these numbers are more than doubled.

Although not nearly so numerous as the Canada geese and pigeons, common pheasants frequent the beech spinneys, feeding in ones and twos on the lawns early or late in the day. The magnificent cock, sporting scarlet wattles around the eyes, typically struts across the lawns calling loudly. Since pheasants repeatedly fall prey to foxes, they are bred and released into the Gardens each year, as part of the ornamental wildfowl collection.

The long-established practice of breeding pheasants for shoots through-out the length and breadth of Britain has ensured that these birds are now very much part of the country scene. Yet there is some doubt as to when they were first introduced to Europe and to Britain from their native southern Asia. Legend has it that they were brought back to Europe by Jason and the Argonauts around 1300 BC. We know from a document held in the British Museum that captive pheasants were certainly kept in Britain

LEFT: *Bar-headed geese in the foregound, Canada geese and ducks behind, weather out a snowstorm during a rare severe winter spell at Kew. A layer of snow has fallen on the partially frozen lake.*

Wildfowl in winter
The Lake
7 February 1991

before the time of the Norman conquest: they are listed (together with black-birds, partridges and geese) as rations for Walton Abbey monastery between Michaelmas 1058 and Ash Wednesday of the following year.

Spectacular avian visitors which cause more than one person to blink on first seeing them are a flock of ring-necked parakeets that roost on the island in the Lake from late summer onwards. This flock has gradually increased in size as escaped birds from various collections have amalgamated. The parakeets probably nest on small islands (known as ayots) in the Thames.

In addition to the wild and feral birds which home in on Kew to feed, to shelter or to breed, the ornamental wildfowl collection is quite extensive. The waterfowl tend to frequent the Lake and its environs, with some moving onto the Pond in front of the Palm House, while the terrestrial wildfowl are more elusive. Both silver and golden pheasants, which originate from Far Eastern forests, occur at Kew, the females a mere shadow of their resplendent mates. Even on the dullest of winter days, the colours of a male golden pheasant are unbelievably brilliant. A survey made at Kew some years ago showed that it was the ornamental wildfowl – rather than the flowers – that had attracted most visitors into the Gardens on that particular day.

There has been a wildfowl collection at Kew since the time when it was a royal estate. As well as the more conventional ducks and geese, pelicans, penguins, peacocks, cranes and storks used to be kept in the Gardens; the storks nested on the mount beside the Temple of Aeolus. A comical sight it may have been to see pelicans dancing on the pansies or the petunias, but no doubt a disheartening one for the gardeners, whose successors in the 1980s faced a similar problem with Canada geese (see p.17).

As the birds in the collection become depleted through natural death as well as predation by foxes, they are supplemented from special breeding pens at Kew not open to the public. From time to time, restocking takes place from the WWT. In return, Kew provides information to the WWT about the breeding status of various wildfowl in the Gardens. The bar-headed goose is breeding well at Kew but, until it is known why this bird's numbers are

BELOW: *One of the few occasions when Canada geese are silenced and static is when they are grounded by a snowstorm. With their bills and long necks tucked into their bodies and covered by a sprinkling of snow, they are remarkably well camouflaged for such large birds.*

Canada geese, Branta canadensis
Rough grass in Woodland Garden
7 February 1991

declining in southern China and northern India where it breeds in the wild, there are no plans to reintroduce it there.

Mute swans are resident in Britain all year round, and wild birds can be seen at Kew during any month, although they usually breed on the River Thames. However, a pair of resident whooper swans had to be returned to the WWT after they developed the disturbing trait of sticking their necks into passing prams! The majestic black swans from Australia, on the other hand, with their spectacular red bills, are a familiar sight on both the Pond and the lawns. Although they built a nest and laid in 1990 and 1991, no eggs hatched.

Many wild ducks – including tufted, pochard, mallard and feral mandarins (from the Duke of Bedford's collection) – swell the wildfowl population, while in very harsh winters large numbers of redwings move in, both to gain shelter and to gorge themselves on plentiful fruits. During a severe spell in February 1991, a flock of waxwings appeared at Kew.

Grey squirrels are much in evidence in autumn, busily foraging beneath trees shedding their fruit, bounding a few metres away, then pausing momentarily to bury their caches in the lawns. The fluffy tail and comical antics make the squirrel doubly appealing, but this alien from North America breeds so successfully that it is now regarded as a pest species in Britain. It is ironic that in 1908, when a pair of grey squirrels was introduced to Kew from Woburn, it was announced that 'Kew is indebted to His Grace the Duke of Bedford for two pairs of American grey squirrels which have been placed in the grounds of Queen's Cottage'. Now these mammals abound in the Gardens and, in some areas where they are regularly fed by visitors, are very approachable. However, not only do they damage the plant collections by debarking trees, but they also have a predilection for chewing plant labels – an essential part of any botanic garden. In addition, they take young birds from their nests and regularly nip over-attentive children. Open-topped rubbish bins were abandoned long ago at Kew but even the tough modern polypropylene bins, complete with lids, are by no means squirrel-proof. Persistent work by sharp incisors means that sooner or later a hole appears in the lid large enough for a squirrel to squeeze through to forage on left-over lunches.

Few people probably appreciate that there is a good bat population in the Gardens, for these small, flying mammals tend to appear late in the day, flitting over the Banks Pond or along the Oak Walk parallel to the River Thames. Unlike the squirrels, bats are positively encouraged by the erection of bat boxes in the Conservation Area, which is not open to the public.

The denser planting of trees in the Conservation Area attracts many birds, including blue and great tits as well as nuthatches and jays. Frequent feeding by visitors has made some tits so tame that they will automatically alight on any outstretched hand, whether it has food on it or not. Late in the day rabbits can be seen munching on the leaves of wild herbaceous plants on open ground, while woodcock come here to overwinter.

During 1912–13, a badger lived in a sett in the grounds of Queen's Cottage, but his partiality to many of the waterfowl collection resulted in his capture and translocation to Essex. Badgers continue to appear spasmodically in the Gardens, while foxes, hedgehogs and moles, as well as various kinds of mice and voles, are all permanent residents.

The Palm House Pond supports a population of fish ranging in size from small sticklebacks to large pike and carp. In June 1906, a carp weighing over 5.4 kilograms (12 lb) was taken from the Pond and given to the Natural History Museum, where it was preserved.

RIGHT: *Even if grey squirrels had not been introduced to Kew early this century, they would, no doubt, have invaded the Gardens naturally. Now there is almost no part where they cannot be seen bounding across the lawns or scrambling up trees, foraging on fruits and nuts as well as left-over lunches:*

Grey squirrel, Sciurus caroliensis, *among bluebells*
Conservation Area
9 May 1991

LEFT: *After foraging for pollen, honeybees return to the entrance of their skep, which is designed in the style of the seventeenth century. Note the coloured pollen loads in the pollen baskets on the last pair of legs.*

Honeybees, Apis mellifera
Queen's Garden
8 June 1991

Insects also abound at Kew, although butterflies would be more numerous if the food plants of their caterpillars were encouraged, since uniform grassy swards are far from appetizing. It is proposed to remedy this shortcoming by maintaining extensive stinging nettle beds. Holly blues, which can be seen on the wing in May – appropriately along Holly Walk – are becoming more plentiful. Butterflies that hibernate during winter, including brimstones, commas, small tortoiseshells and peacocks, can be seen on warmer March days. Later in the year, meadow browns and speckled woods appear in areas of long grass in the Arboretum, while large skippers can be seen feeding on brambles in the Queen's Cottage Garden and, in late autumn, red admirals move in to feed on asters in the Duke's Garden. On sunny days in late summer, grasshoppers can be heard stridulating in rough grassy areas and also in the Grass Garden. There was a time when hawk-eyed visitors to the heated glasshouses could have seen mantids and stick insects lurking in the leafy interiors, but these insects have gradually died out.

Another invertebrate which appears spasmodically in the tropical houses is the flatworm, *Bipalium kewense*, so-named because it was first described from the hothouses at Kew. For some time, it was thought the flatworm was unknowingly transported from Kew to other parts of the world, but an earlier Australian record, predating the Kew discovery by four years, suggests that it is a native of Australia, from where it was brought to Kew in 1878. It has, no doubt, in the past been inadvertently spread from the Gardens to other parts of the world within soil around plant roots. This carnivorous flatworm, with a shovel-shaped head, glides over soil on its mucous trail, feeding on earthworms, insect larvae and snails. The upper surface of the 12-centimetre- ($4\frac{1}{2}$-inch-) long flattened body is yellow ochre with dark stripes, while the underside is greyish-white.

Tucked away beyond a hedge adjacent to the mount topped with a gilded wrought-iron rotunda in the Queen's Garden are two bee hives made from skeps of seventeenth-century design. The 40-centimetre- (15-inch-) high skep

RIGHT: *This, Britain's largest hoverfly, mimics a hornet and is a spasmodic insect visitor to Kew in late summer. In common with smaller hoverflies, the adults visit flowers to feed, giving rise to the alternative name, flower-flies. Hoverfly larvae have quite a different diet; some feed on aphids, while others scavenge on dead pupae inside bee and wasp nests.*

Hoverfly, Volucella zonaria, *feeding on*
  Eryngium monocephalum
Herbaceous Ground
5 August 1989

rests on top of a block of wood with a sliver cut out to allow the bees to fly in and out. Watching honey bees returning to any hive is an interesting exercise, since by no means all of the pollen loads packed in the pollen basket on each hind leg are yellow. While many flowers produce yellow pollen, others produce pollen that is orange (Californian poppy, *Eschscholzia*), red (red dead-nettle, *Lamium purpureum*, and both white and red horsechestnut, *Aesculus* spp.), grey (elm, *Ulmus* procera and broad bean, *Vicia faba*), green (meadow-sweet, *Filipendula ulmaria*), brown (blackthorn, *Prunus spinosa*) and even blue (Siberian squill, *Scilla siberica*, and the dark blue pollen of the oriental poppy, *Papaver orientale*).

Come early summer sawfly larvae, with their characteristic looping motion, may be in evidence on clumps of Solomon's seal, *Polygonatum* sp. In years of heavy infestation they will completely defoliate a large clump, leaving only the main stalk and leaf veins. A more recent insect pest that has invaded gardens in the south-east of England is the lily beetle, *Lilioceris lilii*, a

destructive pest of lilies, which will also attack Solomon's seal, hostas and fritillaries. Widespread in continental Europe and north Africa, the beetle was first recorded in Britain almost a century ago, but it was very rare until 1940 when it was reported in a private garden in Chobham, Surrey. Since then it has spread out in neighbouring counties in south-east England. I first noticed it in my Surrey garden in 1983 but it was not recorded at Kew, some 64 kilometres (40 miles) north, until several years later.

Although only 6–8mm ($\frac{1}{4}$ inch or so) long, the pillar-box red wing cases and thorax of the lily beetle are conspicuous on a green leaf or stem and a closer look reveals a black head, antennae and legs. When held between the fingers, the insect produces a distinctive squeak. The orange-red slug-like larvae rarely appear this colour since they cover their bodies with black, slimy excreta. Both larvae and adults attack leaves, stems, buds and flowers, and all the lily clumps in the Bulb Patio at Kew were infested with lily beetles during the summer of 1991. However, they can be controlled if daily inspections are made and all adults collected. Care needs to be taken when collecting, for the beetles have the disarming habit of suddenly dropping to the ground when disturbed, displaying their dark undersides. If they are allowed to lay their eggs, an infestation soon develops and, when conditions are favourable, they can produce two generations in a year.

As with wild birds, there is always the chance that unusual and exciting insects may appear at Kew from time to time – like the half dozen monarch butterflies, *Danaus plexippus*, seen in 1981, escapees from the London Butterfly House at Syon across the river. They were seen flying along the towpath, in the Queen's Garden and among the Order Beds in the Herbaceous Ground. Here, they had apparently homed straight in on several species of milkweed,

Asclepias, their natural food plant in North America! Eggs were found on *Asclepias incanata, A. syriaca* and *A. speciosa,* but only a few hatched and the young larvae drowned in the early-morning dew. Some eggs were collected and reared by a member of the Kew staff.

The extent of the faunal records published in the *Kew Bulletin* have waxed and waned according to the enthusiasm or special interest of the individual recorder, but one of the most bizarre has to be the bed bug spotted walking across an 'Out' tray in the Herbarium in 1968!

In this chapter, I have focused on some of the wild animals that are attracted to Kew Gardens. The transitory nature of most wildlife means that, unlike the plants, it cannot be precisely pinpointed, but keen-eyed naturalists may well be fortunate enough to spot an unusual visitor simply by being in the right place at the right time.

CHAPTER NINE

FUTURE

Kew has been a major public attraction for over 100 years, but relatively few visitors are aware of its international reputation as a centre for scientific research and conservation. With habitats the world over under threat from industry and developers, Kew has an increasingly important role to play in saving endangered plant species from extinction.

WITHOUT GREEN plants, man and other animals cannot exist. Our food originates either directly from plants or via herbivorous animals that have been domesticated. Peoples who traditionally live an outdoor existence are acutely aware of the value of plants: they depend on them not only for food, but also for clothing and cures for disease and illness. Indeed, herbal medicine stalls can still be seen in markets throughout China, a country where over 5,000 medicinal plants have been documented.

Yet, by the continued felling of natural forests, man is reducing this largely untapped reservoir of natural products and remedies. Large-scale clearance of forests, indiscriminate use of pesticides, draining and infilling of wetlands, and ploughing of grasslands: all these activities are eroding the biological diversity – the variety of life on earth – whether it be on a genetic, species or habitat level.

In addition to directly destroying habitats, man is also endangering many species and their habitats indirectly through pollution. In recent years there has been a progressive deterioration in the health of temperate forests and freshwater lakes showered by acid rain, resulting from atmospheric pollution by sulphur dioxide and nitrous oxide emissions. But now one of the most serious threats to life on earth, as we know it, is climatic change

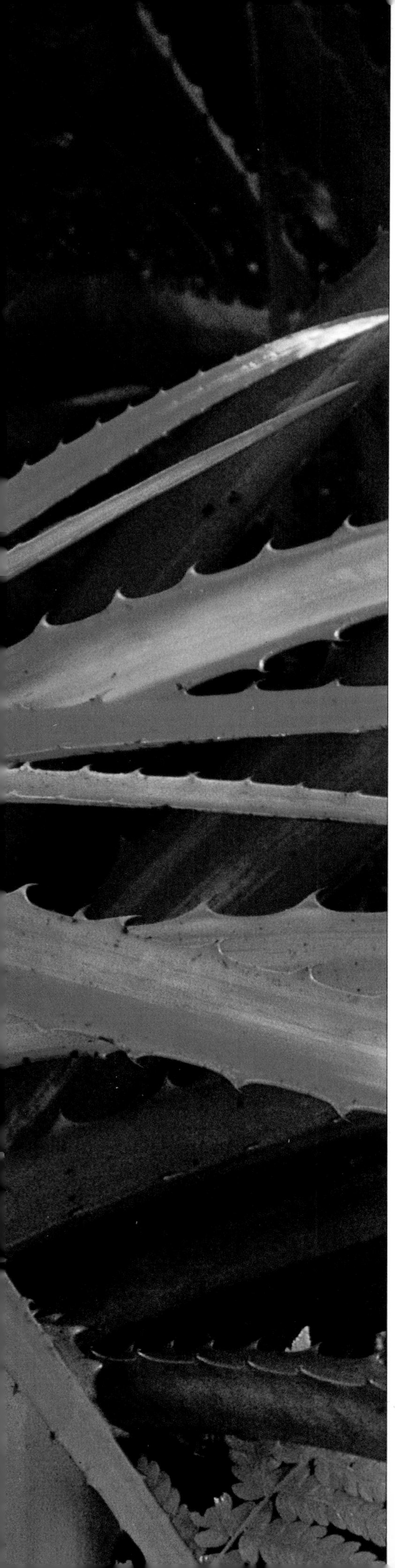

LEFT: *Many examples of a radially symmetrical design can be seen among the bromeliad collection in the Princess of Wales Conservatory. Bromeliads tend to have their leaves arranged in the form of a rosette. Most have small and rather insignificant flowers, which are greatly enhanced by colourful bracts as shown here by* Bromelia serra.

LEFT: *The Japanese banana produces inedible fruit, but the fibre from the leaf stalks is used for making durable cloth and sails. It flowers and fruits freely in the Temperate House over a period of several months. A related species from the Philippines,* Musa textilis, *produces manila hemp used in the shipping industry for mooring ropes.*

Japanese banana, Musa bashoo
Temperate House
25 August 1991

brought about by global warming caused by atmospheric increases in greenhouse gases such as carbon dioxide and methane. We tend to think of global warming solely in terms of increases in air and sea temperatures, but rising sea levels would also flood the habitats of many wild plants while, further inland, the soil's moisture content would be reduced. Plants, apparently safe in protected areas, would no longer be immune to such drastic climatic changes.

If habitats continue to be destroyed at the present rate, it is estimated that more than a tenth of the world's plant species will be extinct within the next decade. The loss of potential resources is highlighted by noting that less than 5 per cent of the known quarter of a million flowering plants have been tested for their pharmaceutical value. Even though we depend on very few plants for the bulk of our food (twenty kinds provide 90 per cent of our nutrition), we need to maintain as wide a variety of natural habitats as possible, otherwise imbalances in natural cycles will result. Plants cannot be considered in isolation from animals. Not only do animals depend on plants for their food, but many plants often depend on animals either to pollinate their flowers or to disperse their fruits.

Conservation of plants in the wild (*in situ*) through protection of habitats by the setting up of National Parks and other types of reserve is admirable, provided that they are adequately wardened. By means of both scientific research and education, The Royal Botanic Gardens, Kew, are striving not only to reduce, but also to reverse, the rate at which habitats and their plants are being destroyed worldwide. Kew, together with other botanic gardens, is now playing an increasingly important role in the conservation of species outside their habitats (*ex-situ* conservation). They are acting as custodians of threatened species and, in some cases, propagating them for possible re-introduction to the wild. Each year, plant-hunting expeditions from Kew continue to bring back live plants and herbarium specimens. The live plants are kept in a quarantine house, to make sure that no pests have been inadvertently introduced, before they are transferred to a nursery glasshouse. Rare plants are propagated here so that they can be distributed to other botanical centres.

Seed, too, is collected from wild plants for Kew's Seed Bank at Wakehurst Place in Sussex which now holds seeds from some 3,500 species, notably those from habitats which are under threat. By reducing the moisture content of seeds from plants of temperate and semi-arid regions to a mere 5 per cent and also lowering the temperature to −20°C (−4°F), it is possible to store them for decades. Kew is working in collaboration with English Nature ultimately to store seed of species of British wild flowering plants. Initially, the aim has been to concentrate on the most endangered species. Seeds of rainforest and aquatic plants present much more of a problem, for they do not survive being dried. Such difficult subjects are therefore being investigated by the Seed Research Group at Wakehurst Place.

BELOW: *The highly textured leaves of the perennial* Boehmeria biloba *make it an excellent foliage plant, but it has a limited distribution outdoors, since it is not hardy. This member of the nettle family grows on rocky shores on the coast of Japan. A related species,* Boehmeria nivea – *the Chinese silk plant or ramie – produces the largest, strongest and silkiest vegetable fibres known, eight times stronger than cotton. Widely cultivated in China, it is woven into clothes and used for fishing nets, sacking and also gas mantles.*

Boehmeria biloba
Temperate House
27 July 1991

Since October 1968 every plant which has arrived at Kew has been given a ten-figure 'accession' number. These numbers can be seen on many of the plant labels in the Gardens, although not on the older trees which were planted long before the system came into operation. Each number is logged into a computer database together with information about the location in which the plant was growing in the wild. All this aids horticulturists to simulate the optimal conditions required by each plant if it is to be grown successfully at Kew.

For most of this century successive government bodies, from the Board of Agriculture to the Ministry of Agriculture, Fisheries and Food, have funded the operation of Kew. On 1 April 1984 the responsibility was transferred, under the terms of the National Heritage Act 1983, to a Board of Trustees. Although it is still grant-aided, Kew now has to supplement a proportion of the income which it needs in order to maintain and run the Gardens from other sources.

Visitors now pay a more realistic entrance fee to enjoy and benefit from these unique Gardens. In return, the service to visitors is steadily being improved. For example, there is much more information available about many of the plants and their natural habitats. In recent years much greater emphasis has been placed on increasing public knowledge and awareness of the significance and importance of plants, at the same time advertising the key role of the work at The Royal Botanic Gardens, Kew.

Self-guided special-interest trails are also being devised. The Japanese Plants Trail (1991) introduces the visitor to the many Japanese plants at Kew, growing not only in the main glasshouses but also scattered throughout the Arboretum. Plants highlighted along the Princess of Wales Mathematics Trail, devised in 1992, are of interest because of their natural designs which include radial symmetry or spiral and polygonal forms.

Spring 1992 saw the launch of a scheme whereby some twenty Kew Guides, a body of volunteers, conduct pre-booked tours as well as timetabled tours for those visitors who prefer to be guided around part of the extensive grounds. It is planned to widen the scope to include special-interest tours. Training days run for teachers, with the provision of teachers' packs, help them to devise projects which will be most relevant to their own pupils when they visit Kew. Few British schoolchildren are able to experience rainforests or coral reefs at first hand, so even a short visit to the Palm House gives them some insight into the conditions necessary for rainforest plants and tropical marine algae to flourish. Each summer vacation a few fortunate art students come to Kew to gain experience in portraying the shapes and textures of unfamiliar exotic plants. Their illustrations are often reproduced in the numerous leaflets and publications designed by the Media Resources Unit each year. The unit also uses the Cibachrome process for reproducing high-resolution authentic colour prints of herbarium sheets. These can then be sent to scientists anywhere in the world, without risk of damage or loss to the original specimens.

Adult education is also expanding at Kew, with several regular long and short courses. The Kew School of Garden Design is a five-week course repeated three times during the year which attracts students from all over the world. Other courses open to members of the public include Conservation Techniques, Botanical Illustration and Plant Photography. In addition there are one-day workshops and lectures on botanical, horticultural and environmental topics.

ABOVE: *The Madagascar periwinkle is just one of many rainforest plants that have been found to contain life-saving drugs – in this case the substances vincristine and vinblastine, which improve the remission rates of Hodgkin's disease and childhood leukaemia. Often mistaken for a busy lizzie (Impatiens), the Madagascar periwinkle belongs to an entirely different family and is frequently used as an ornamental plant in tropical gardens.*

Madagascar periwinkle, Catharanthus
  roseus
Palm House
12 June 1991

RIGHT: Streptocarpus *is a genus native to tropical and South Africa as well as Madagascar, Burma and Thailand. These attractive, but non-hardy plants have to be grown under glass in Britain. S. rexii, which flowered at Kew Gardens in 1827, was the first* Streptocarpus *to bloom in cultivation. When this species was cross-pollinated with S. dunnii in 1886, the garden hybrid illustrated here was produced.*

Streptocarpus × kewensis
Floral display, Princess of Wales
  Conservatory
2 June 1991

While some of these activities are self-supporting or even profitable, additional funds have to be found. The Kew Foundation was set up in 1990 with the aim of attracting corporate bodies to sponsor specific scientific, educational and amenity projects. Individuals have the opportunity to contribute to the maintenance of the gardens at Kew and Wakehurst Place, and the funding of scientific research at the former, by becoming a Friend of The Royal Botanic Gardens, Kew.

Student gardeners have worked and trained at Kew since 1859 when Sir Joseph Hooker introduced evening lectures during their two-year course. This was initially confined to men students, but women were permitted to join the course in 1896. At this time the days were long and arduous, beginning at 6 a.m., and even after attending a lecture ending at 8 p.m. students were expected to continue working in the Library. Gradually the hours of garden work were reduced and the number of lectures increased. In 1963 the prestigious three-year Kew Diploma Course, providing a broad-based training in amenity horticulture, was initiated. Now run by the School of Horticulture, it attracts students from all over the world.

This book highlights some of the many plants on view at Kew, considering them not in isolation but rather as part of a habitat or geographic region where they naturally occur. Indeed, in recent years, whenever the opportunity has arisen, such as during reconstruction of the Rock Garden or after renovation of an old glasshouse or building a new one, plants have been rearranged under natural geographic areas or habitat types, instead of being displayed simply as collections of individual specimens.

As we move towards the twenty-first century and natural habitats unaffected by man's activities continue to grow rarer, so the research done at Kew, expanding the knowledge of biodiversity, will be crucial. Kew's annual target for the addition or replacement of wild-origin plants to the Gardens is 4,000, plus the addition of 1,500 accessions of live seed to the wild Seed Bank. As the collections increase, it is likely that more plants with life-saving properties will be discovered. As an example, the seeds and leaves of the Moreton Bay chestnut, *Castanospermum australe*, a plant of Australian rainforests, has been found to contain a substance that reduces the infectious nature of the AIDS virus. What is more, the same substance was discovered in a pod of a plant from the Central American forests which had been stored in the Herbarium for forty years!

A recent discovery in the laboratories at Kew has been the isolation of a chemical present in the leaves and roots of bugles, *Ajuga* spp., which is a powerful insecticide. When scientists noticed there were very few insects feeding on the plants, they decided to analyse the chemicals inside them. The natural insecticide appears to inhibit feeding by insect pests, leaving them weak and also infertile. The research being carried out at Kew is part of an intensive worldwide effort to discover natural chemicals that can be used in preference to man-made ones.

In addition, by using micro-propagation techniques, Kew is playing a major role in the conservation of rare plants in cultivation. Re-introduction of rare plants into the wild is, however, proving more problematical since good field botanists are required to monitor their condition and perhaps even to warden them. Wild orchids have already been re-introduced to several British locations (see p.124) and plants of *Globularia sarcophylla* raised at Kew are being grown in the botanic garden on the island of Gran Canaria as a half-way house before their re-introduction to the wild there.

Spirals are widespread in nature. The most common examples are the new fronds of ferns and tendrils of climbing plants. Young fronds of Cibotium *tree ferns are covered with golden-brown hairs, which were once used for dressing wounds in China.* Costus *is a group of tropical herbs belonging to the ginger family.*

ABOVE: *Tight spiral of new* Cibotium glaucum *frond*
15 June 1991

RIGHT: *Loose spiral of* Costus verschaffeltanus
27 June 1991
Princess of Wales Conservatory

As the world's largest collection of living wild-origin plants continues to expand and methods of interpreting them is extended, so the pleasure for visitors to Kew is enhanced. Within 13 kilometres (8 miles) of the centre of London visitors can, in a single day, focus on the flora from habitats as diverse as tropical rainforests, deserts and coral reefs. This experience must help to promote awareness – as well as appreciation – of plants on a world scale and of the pressing need to contribute towards their conservation.

MAP OF KEW GARDENS

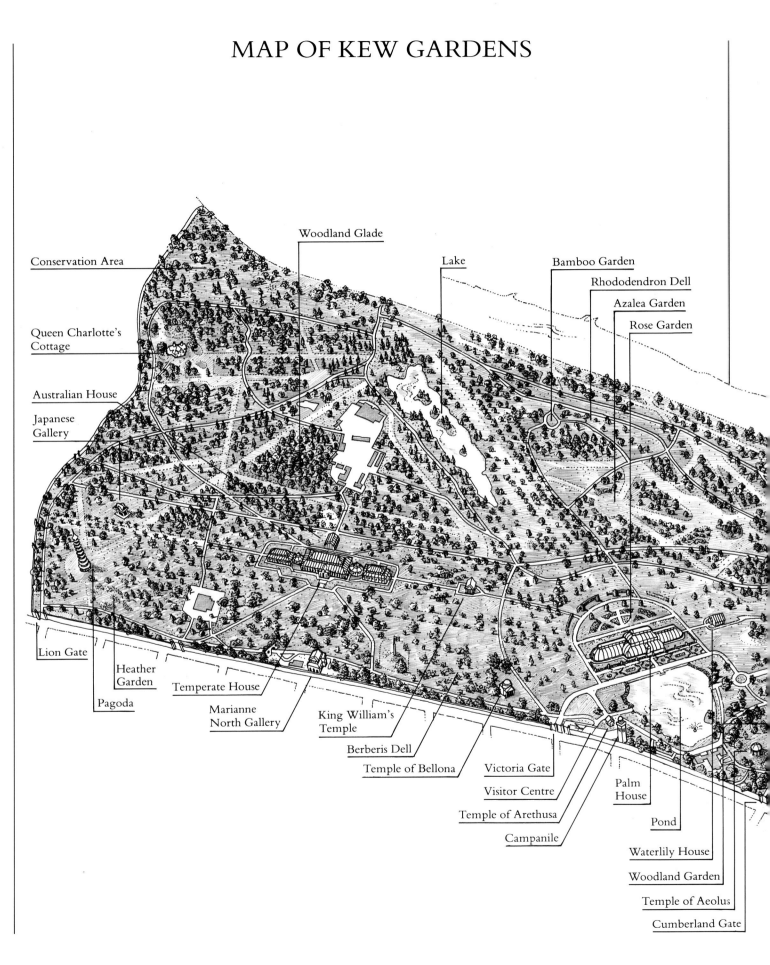

Conservation Area

Woodland Glade

Lake

Bamboo Garden

Rhododendron Dell

Azalea Garden

Rose Garden

Queen Charlotte's
Cottage

Australian House

Japanese
Gallery

Lion Gate

Heather
Garden

Pagoda

Temperate House

Marianne
North Gallery

King William's
Temple

Berberis Dell

Temple of Bellona

Victoria Gate

Visitor Centre

Temple of Arethusa

Campanile

Palm
House

Pond

Waterlily House

Woodland Garden

Temple of Aeolus

Cumberland Gate

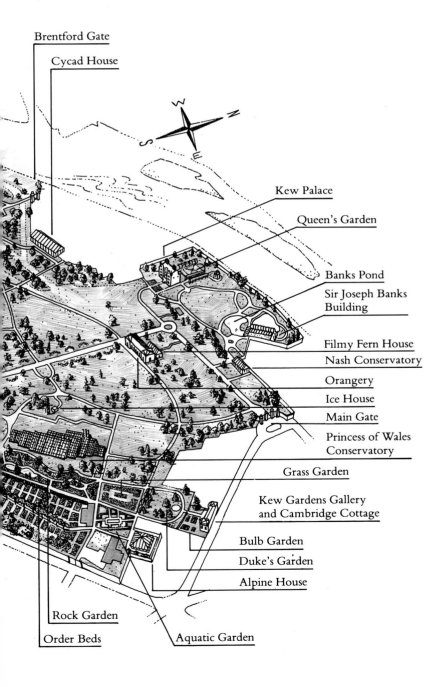

Brentford Gate

Cycad House

Kew Palace

Queen's Garden

Banks Pond

Sir Joseph Banks
Building

Filmy Fern House

Nash Conservatory

Orangery

Ice House

Main Gate

Princess of Wales
Conservatory

Grass Garden

Kew Gardens Gallery
and Cambridge Cottage

Bulb Garden

Duke's Garden

Alpine House

Rock Garden

Order Beds

Aquatic Garden

PHOTOGRAPHIC NOTES

To many people, plant photography appears deceptively easy since, unlike animals, the subjects are fixed – if not always static. However, successful pictures depend on many factors, not least the weather (notoriously fickle in island Britain) and the condition of the plants themselves. Although it is well nigh impossible to distil the art of plant photography into just a few pages, the following notes on how I tackled this project may be of interest to photography enthusiasts.

CLIMATIC EXTREMES

During the period when the majority of pictures were taken for this book, Kew experienced several spells of abnormal weather. The year 1990 began with gale-force winds in January which felled or damaged beyond repair 120 trees at Kew (less than three years after the devastating October 1987 gale); then there was a very warm, early spring followed by late frosts which destroyed much new growth (notably among the lilacs). The summer of 1990 was so hot that the extensive green lawns became parched and yellow, precluding any chance of taking scenic vistas until the rains fell. Flowers quickly fade in hot weather, so perfectly shaped blooms have to be photographed without delay.

Snow rarely settles at Kew, for London's micro-climate keeps the ambient temperature a few degrees above that of the surrounding areas. The early part of 1991 therefore proved a bonus when snow settled over two periods, providing scope for some traditional winter shots. Come the summer, June turned out to be one of the wettest on record. Whereas light rain can prolong the life of flowers, heavy rain not only weighs down branches but can also spoil flowers by causing spotting on the petals.

SUBJECT SELECTION

Producing stereotyped pictures from a clear-cut brief, with a list of species that can be ticked off, makes the photographer's job easy since you simply work through the list until it is complete. However, everyone agreed that such an approach would not be suitable for this particular book, since it would inevitably result in many straightforward record plant portraits. Ideally, the plants should be photographed as and when they appear especially photogenic. Yet, I soon found that having access to 120 hectares (300 acres), with 37,000 species of plants, proved daunting to say the least. Where do you begin? For one thing, obtaining striking plant pictures is not a question of applying a specific formula. It may involve luck; invariably it will take effort and time – time in casting a perceptive eye to select a perfect (and accessible) specimen or waiting for the optimum lighting (or perhaps modifying it in some way).

Two approaches were adopted. First, I photographed anything which caught my eye because of the way it was lit or because of its texture or pattern. Second, I did a lot of homework. I spoke to people who alerted me to subjects worth considering. Also, whenever I saw a plant that I knew to be particularly interesting, I made a note to return when it would be at its best – when it was flowering, fruiting, or maybe turning colour in autumn.

However long the day, it was quite impossible to cover more than a small area of the Gardens, so that sometimes, when I returned to a glasshouse, I

LEFT: *As I entered the Queen's Garden, the teasel seedheads, backlit by the low-angled sun, immediately caught my eye. I tried getting closer with a shorter lens, but found the best camera angle with the simplest background was from further back with a long telephoto lens.*

Teasel, Dipsacus sylvestris *with 200–400 mm lens*
Queen's Garden
21 August 1991

BELOW: *A low-angled sun also helped to hightlight a portrait of a peony flower. By selecting an overhead viewpoint, I was able to take advantage of the side lighting grazing across the petals so that they appeared to glow.*

Paeonia mollis *with 105 mm macro lens*
Herbaceous Ground
14 May 1992

found that plants in bud just a short time before had bloomed and faded. On the other hand, many glasshouse staff made a point of letting me know where and when I would be able to find a plant with a particularly spectacular flower or fruit.

A glance at the date given in each picture caption will show that some days proved to be much more productive than others. Surprisingly, the clemency of the weather and the length of time spent in the Gardens bore little relation to the number of acceptable pictures achieved.

At first sight, there may appear to be some obvious omissions. For example, some of the best-known tropical flowers such as bougainvillea and frangipani, as well as temperate cultivars such as hybrid tea roses and lilacs, have been excluded in preference to other specimens which are perhaps less familiar. It is hoped that these pictures may encourage readers to seek out and see plants for themselves.

EQUIPMENT

I used two different camera systems: the medium format Hasselblad and the 35mm format Nikon F4. I favoured the Hasselblad for scenics and larger plant portraits (using 60, 80, 150 and 250mm lenses on the 500 C/M body as well as the Superwide model with the fixed 38mm lens), and the Nikon for close-ups and all wildlife studies. The Nikon lenses I used for the plates reproduced in this book ranged from 20mm to 500mm – although the 500mm was used solely for taking some of the more timid wildlife subjects.

From experience, I know that it is unwise to be dogmatic about specifying a particular lens for a particular subject; however, general guidelines may be useful. For taking views and vistas, a wide-angle lens is most appropriate and, in situations where the camera had to be tilted down (from a raised walkway) or up, I used a perspective correcting lens to straighten the converging verticals. A standard 50mm or a short telephoto – such as an 85mm – is suitable for photographing specimen trees, and a macro lens, with its own inbuilt extension, is essential for close-up studies of bark, leaves, flowers or fruits. I use both 105mm and 200mm macro lenses for taking close-ups out in the open and under glass.

Because I spend a great deal of time photographing wildlife all over the world, I have a wide range of telephoto lenses. Although I would not normally recommend a lens as long as 400mm for taking flower portraits, I found the Nikkor ED 200–400mm zoom useful for isolating larger flowers growing under glass from unsightly background struts and glass panes (see the crane flower on p.oo) or for making elevated flowers accessible (such as the cedar cones on p.oo). When I focused it on waterlily blooms in the aquatic garden, however, it revealed a heavy infestation of aphids not apparent to the naked eye! It was also useful for throwing distracting backgrounds in the gardens out of focus (see the grasses on p.oo and the teasel heads on p.oo). Calico flowers growing high up in the Palm House (see p.oo) proved impossible to photograph as detailed close-ups from ground level, even with the longest lens, but an offer of a ride in the hydraulic lift used for high-level pruning solved the problem in a matter of minutes.

Without exception, every picture was taken by supporting the camera with the highly versatile Benbo tripod. Permission must be obtained from the Public Relations Section to use a tripod (or an artist's easel) at Kew. All professional photographers have to apply for permission to photograph at Kew, with or without a tripod.

ABOVE: *Dark-leaved plants can be difficult to photograph successfully because automatic meters tend to over-expose a darker than average tone. In low light levels there is always the temptation to use flash, but I preferred to use the natural light filtering through the glass.*

Begonia serrati petala *with 105 mm macro lens*
Princess of Wales Conservatory, Tropical Ferns Section
27 June 1991

Working on such a level site was perfect for using a shopping trolley to transport all my photographic equipment around the Gardens. Initially, I used a basic model, until I found one with a collapsible seat, which meant that I was reasonably comfortable during the time spent waiting for wild birds to appear, as I could set up a camera with a long lens on a tripod and sit down to survey the scene.

LIGHTING

One of the easiest ways of photographing plants is when they are lit from the front, but varying the direction of the lighting can produce far more interesting pictures. Examples of plants lit by available light from different directions can be seen among the plates from the side (Venus flytrap on p.72), from the front (yucca outside the Princess of Wales Conservatory on p.91) and from behind (beech leaves on p.29 and Catalpa pods with the Temperate House on p.23). In the latter case, the distinctive pods show no colour, for they are seen as silhouettes because the exposure was metered from the lighter sky behind. Overcast days with a light or heavy cloud cover produce soft indirect lighting, which is particularly appropriate for taking white and pastel-coloured subjects such as the Christmas roses in snow on p.15.

If the natural lighting is not ideal, it can often be modified or enhanced in several ways, especially for close-ups. For example, light can be deflected on to a subject in shadow by using a reflector. A silver one gives more natural lighting than a gold finish which produces a warm cast. I use circular Lastolite reflectors, but a piece of cooking foil wrapped around board is just as effective.

The development of dedicated electronic flash guns which meter the light directly off the film plane means that photographing a non-static plant in poor light on an overcast day is no longer a problem with slow-speed film. Several plates in this book (including the red meconopsis on p.109 and the Sterculia fruit on p.54) were taken using the fill-flash technique whereby the flash is balanced for the daylight reading (though I generally prefer to under-expose the flash by $\frac{2}{3}$–1 stop to ensure this light is not obviously apparent). This obviates the problem of an unlit, nocturnal-looking background which occurs when flash is used as the prime light source. Fill-flash is also invaluable when using a long focus lens for taking high-level subjects lit by dappled lighting, which light bounced from a reflector cannot reach. Because I very rarely choose to light a plant from the front, I use the Nikon SB–24 flash connected to the hot shoe on the F4 camera, by means of a flash sync cord. In this way, I can hold the flash out to one side, above or even behind the plant. Fill-flash should not be used for taking moving subjects with an exposure longer than $\frac{1}{8}$ second, because this will result in an obvious ghost image in which the subject continues to move after the short duration of the flash.

While direct sunlight can add depth to a general view by creating shadows and can produce dramatic effects by rim-lighting a solid subject or trans-illuminating large, coloured petals or autumnal leaves, it is far from ideal when you are photographing white or pastel-coloured flowers. If the sun persists, the intensity of the light can be reduced by holding a white diffuser between it and the subject (a sheet of muslin will do) to soften both the light and the shadows in a similar way to a light cloud cover over the sun.

The picture of the backlit teasel heads, on p.151, is an example of an unplanned picture found purely by chance, simply by being in the right place at the right time. I looked at a closer view with a shorter lens, but decided the best result would be to stand further back and shoot with a long focus lens.

As I was walking out of the Palm House one day, I looked up and saw this attractive design created by the leaf mosaic of the paw-paw. The only way I could get this shot was by crouching on the floor and using a very wide-angle lens.

Paw-paw Carica papaya *with*
20 mm lens
Palm House
11 October 1991

Many blue flowers are notoriously difficult to reproduce authentically – as we see them – on colour film. The reason is that they reflect some far red and infra-red wavelengths that we cannot see, but which some colour films reproduce. In spring 1991, I photographed bluebells using a variety of colour transparency films. These trials showed that the blueness was enhanced by indirect sunlight (where plants grew in the shadow of trees or when open-grown clumps were taken on a cloudy day) and by using flash for close-ups. Indeed, it can be preferable to eliminate direct sunlight falling on blue flowers by casting a shadow and then adding some sparkle by using fill-flash. While a blue colour-correcting (20CC blue) gelatin filter placed over the lens helped to enhance the blueness of blue flowers, it did produce a cold, blue-green colour to all green stems and leaves included in the frame. I found the most natural colours were achieved using Ektachrome 100-Plus film with available light.

GLASSHOUSES

Photography in hot and humid glasshouses presents the added problem of cold camera lenses and viewfinders (not to mention spectacles) steaming up.

LEFT AND ABOVE: *This pair of pictures of the same plant – taken two years apart – show the variable conditions that can exist at the same time of year in the wet tropical environment recreated at Kew. The shot on the left shows more colour, but I prefer the muted colours in the atmospheric shot above.*

Portea petropolitana *with 105 mm macro lens (left) and with 80 mm lens on Hasselblad (above).*
Princess of Wales Conservatory, Wet Tropics Section
8 June 1991 and 26 June 1989

Wiping away the condensation with a lens cloth is not the answer, for the glass surfaces simply steam up again. The only solution is to take the cameras and lenses out of the gadget bag as soon as you enter a hot house and wait some fifteen minutes for the condensation gradually to evaporate as the equipment warms up to the ambient temperature. If a picture is taken before the lens clears, it will appear soft, lacking both crispness and contrast – the same effect as if it had been taken with a soft-focus filter (indeed, some portrait photographers breathe on a lens to produce an ephemeral soft-focus filter to help to soften wrinkles in an ageing face).

In spite of this inconvenience, I found myself very much attracted to both the Wet Tropics section of the Princess of Wales Conservatory and the Palm House and 20 per cent of the pictures selected for this book were taken in these humid tropical environments. I used the time spent waiting for lenses to clear to check which plants were worth photographing.

Other problems associated with working in any glasshouse – heated or not – include shadows cast by glazing bars and white deposits appearing on shiny leaves, notably camellias, from repeated watering. Shadows will disappear when direct sunlight is softened by a cloud; while powdery deposits on leaves in a privately owned glasshouse can be removed by wiping the leaves with a cloth soaked in olive oil.

Occasionally there are distinct bonuses to be gained when working under glass. Take, for example, the evocative misty atmosphere with the tree fern (p.45) photographed early in the morning after the Wet Tropics section had been doused with hoses on a scorching midsummer's day. The steamy atmosphere conveys to perfection a humid rainforest environment. Then, on two separate visits to the Palm House, I was attracted by plants which sparkled with water drops from recent spraying – the velvet banana (p.54) and Barbados pride (p.20).

AQUARIUM PHOTOGRAPHY

Unless special precautions are taken, additional problems arise when photographing through glass – for example, the small tanks in the Princess of Wales Conservatory and the large ones in the Marine Display in the basement of the Palm House. First, although the tanks are lit with metal halide strip lights which produce acceptable colours on daylight transparency film, flash is needed to freeze all movement of fish and swaying submerged plants or algae. However, if a flash attached to the camera is used, it will be reflected straight off the front glass and back into the lens, thereby ruining the picture. So the flash (connected by a flash sync extension lead) must be held to one side of the camera, angled into the glass at about 45°.

The second problem is that any pale-toned objects – be they hands, white clothing or white lettering around the lens barrel – will appear in the picture as reflections in the front glass when the camera is held away from the tank. If a rubber lens hood is used and the lettering covered with matt black tape, the camera can be held flush against the glass without any risk of scratching it and the reflections will not appear in the picture.

If, however, the camera has to be held well away from the glass in order to get a wider field of view then a matt black board mask with a hole cut out of the centre will have to be attached to the front of the lens. Either a glassless filter ring or an adaptor for a Hoya or Cokin filter system, glued to the back of the board around the hole, can be fixed securely to the front of the camera lens.

BELOW: *An electronic flash was used to freeze the movement of the sea horse in one of the tanks in the Marine Display. Reflections of the camera, hands and flash were eliminated by attaching a black cardboard mask to the front of the lens.*

Sea horse, Hippocampus *sp. with green alga* Halimeda *with 105 mm macro lens Palm House, Marine Display*
4 June 1991

GLOSSARY

ANNUAL A plant that completes its life cycle (germinates, flowers, fruits and sets seed) within a 12-month period.

ANTHER The terminal part of a **stamen** containing the pollen.

AREOLE A cushion-like structure found in cacti, from which spines, hairs and flowers arise.

ARIL The coloured fleshy outgrowth from or around the seed of some plants, e.g. yew.

BULBIL A small bulb produced in a leaf axil (the angle where a leaf or leaf-stalk joins the stem) or in an **inflorescence**.

CALYX The outer part of a flower, often green or brown, made up of **sepals**, which protects the unopened flower bud.

CAULIFLORY The production of flowers (and fruits) directly on the trunk or branches of some tropical trees, e.g. cocoa.

CLADODE A green, flattened leaf-like stem which functions as a leaf.

CULM The flowering stem of a grass.

CULTIVAR A variant that is of value as a garden plant, and which may arise in cultivation or be brought in from the wild. Cultivar names are given after the botanical name in quotes, e.g. *Fagus sylvatica* 'Pendula'.

DICOTYLEDON A member of a large group (class) of flowering plants which produce two seed leaves (cotyledons) in embryo. Later leaves usually have a network of veins. The flower parts are usually in multiples of four or five. The group includes most broad-leaved plants. See **monocotyledon**.

DIPTEROCARP A family of evergreen tropical trees, chiefly from Indo-Malaysia. Many dipterocarps are important timber trees. Some have **sepals** which grow out to form wings on the fruit that aid wind dispersal.

EPIPHYTE A plant that grows on another (larger) plant without being parasitic on it, e.g. some lichens, mosses, ferns, bromeliads and orchids.

EUTROPHICATION The process whereby organic matter in nutrient-rich freshwater bodies increases to a higher level than usual.

GYMNOSPERM A member of a group of seed plants that have unenclosed ovules (which develop into seeds after fertilization) e.g. conifers, cycads, ginkgo.

INFLORESCENCE A number of flowers grouped together into a unit.

LEAF MOSAIC The arrangement of leaves on the branches of a tree when viewed against the sky.

LEGUME The fruit (pod) of plants belonging to the pea family, which usually splits into two halves.

MONOCOTYLEDON The smaller of two groups (classes) of flowering plants, each of which produce a single seed-leaf (cotyledon) in embryo. The leaves have parallel veins. The flower parts are usually in multiples of three. Cereals, grasses, bamboos, bananas, palms, daffodils, lilies, tulips and orchids are all examples of monocotyledons. See **dicotyledon**.

MONTANE Appertaining to mountains.

MUCILAGE A gelatinous substance produced by plants.

MYCHORRHIZA A symbiotic association of the roots of a green plant with a fungus.

NODE The joint of a stem where one or more leaves (or bracts) arise.

PALMATE Describes a leaf with more than three leaflets arising from same point, like the fingers of a hand.

PANICLE A branched **inflorescence**, especially one on which the youngest flowers are closest to the tip.

PAPPUS Hairs developed from the **calyx** around fruits. The hairs act like a parachute, aiding wind dispersal, e.g. in dandelions and thistles.

PERENNIAL A plant that lives for more than two years, usually flowering each year, e.g. delphinium (herbaceous perennial). Shrubs and trees are woody perennials.

PERFOLIATE Describes a pair of stalkless opposite leaves joined at their bases.

PINNATE Describes a leaf in which leaflets are arranged in opposite pairs on each side of the leaf stalk, e.g. ash, ferns.

RHIZOME A horizontal stem, underground or on the surface, from which roots and shoots arise. Some, e.g. irises, are fleshy storage organs; others, e.g. grasses, provide a quick way of spreading.

SEPAL The separate outer protective parts of a flower, often green or brown but may be coloured, together known as a **calyx**.

STAMEN The male part of a flower that bears the pollen.

STOMATA Microscopic pores, usually on the underside of leaves, through which gaseous exchange takes place.

SUCCULENT A fleshy plant which stores water in modified leaves or stems; this group includes many **xerophytic** plants.

TILLER A side shoot of a grass arising at ground level.

TUBER A thickened, swollen stem or root, usually underground, that stores food reserves for a plant, e.g. dahlia, begonia, cyclamen.

UMBEL An **inflorescence** in which all flower stalks arise from the top of the main stem to form an umbrella-shaped compound flower head; hence, the family name Umbelliferae (carrot family), which includes hogweed and fennel.

XEROPHYTE A plant that is tolerant of dry conditions.

INDEX

ACKNOWLEDGEMENTS

The following companies, organizations and individuals kindly assisted me in researching the text or obtaining pictures for this book: British Trust for Ornithology; Children's Tropical Forest, UK; Civil Airports Authority; Copersucar, Brazil; Department of Trade and Industry; English Nature; Forestry Commission; Hensby Biotech Ltd; Ministry of Agriculture, Fisheries and Food; Natural History Museum, London; *New Scientist*; Dennis Orchard Duplicates; Michael and Jan Ramscar; Dave and Val Richards; Royal Horticultural Society; St Mary's Hospital, London, Mycology Department; Studio Import and Marketing Ltd; Worldwide Fund for Nature.

I should especially like to thank the Director and Staff of The Royal Botanic Gardens, Kew; in particular Brinsley Burbidge, who heads the Education and Marketing Department, for initiating the idea of this book, and Valerie Walley, Commercial Development Manager, who thereafter smoothed my passage, meeting my innumerable requests. Special thanks go also to Gail Bromley, Education Manager, and Laura Ponsonby, Education Officer, who initially guided me towards many plants of interest and helped with queries throughout. Sandra Bell, Dave Cook, Rupert Hastings, Jim Keesing, Mike Maunder and Pete Morris were a tremendous help too. In addition my thanks are due to the staff of Kew Library and many other Kew staff who cheerfully answered my endless queries, while the staff working with the Living Collections on display and in the Nursery all helped me achieve the pictures I wanted.

I am also grateful to Sue Corkhill for deciphering and converting my handwritten script into an immaculate manuscript and for typing endless captions, while Rona Tiller and Jackie Woodhams both assisted on the secretarial and editorial side. My mother, Hazel Le Rougetel, read and commented most constructively on the complete manuscript and Louise Bustard and Joyce Stewart read and commented on selected parts, as well as showing me plants of interest. As always my husband, Martin Angel, was a constant source of encouragement. I am indebted to the editorial and design team at Collins & Brown for their attention to detail – in particular to Sarah Hoggett on the editorial side. The result is a most attractively produced book, with colour reproductions that bring to life so vividly the world of plants to be found at Kew.